D1130607

8-7-63    22-5116

# THE WORD IN WORSHIP

# THE WORD IN WORSHIP

## PREACHING AND ITS SETTING
## IN COMMON WORSHIP

*by*

## THOMAS H. KEIR

*Minister of Melrose St. Cuthbert's*
*Parish Church*

LONDON

OXFORD UNIVERSITY PRESS

NEW YORK          TORONTO

1962

*Oxford University Press, Amen House, London E.C.4*

GLASGOW  NEW YORK  TORONTO  MELBOURNE  WELLINGTON
BOMBAY  CALCUTTA  MADRAS  KARACHI  LAHORE  DACCA
CAPE TOWN  SALISBURY  NAIROBI  IBADAN  ACCRA
KUALA LUMPUR  HONG KONG

PRINTED IN GREAT BRITAIN

# PREFACE

The chapters which follow are an expansion of the five Warrack Lectures (the Preacher's Lectureship) for 1960, which were delivered in Christ's College, Aberdeen, and Trinity College, Glasgow. For obvious reasons the pattern of the lectures has been faithfully retained in the volume, even while a certain amount of additional material has been added.

I must acknowledge the courtesy of the General Assembly's Committee for the Training of the Ministry in nominating me for this lectureship, of the General Assembly of the Church of Scotland in sustaining the nomination, and also of the colleges whose hospitality was generously offered.

The Committee suggested that I might, if the proposal commended itself, deal with the ever important concern of preaching in relation to its liturgical context, in the setting, that is to say, of public worship including both prayer and the Church's song. In accepting this proposal I make no claim to be a liturgiologist in the full sense. My business has been to lead the common worship of the Church rather than to specialize in its endlessly proliferated forms.

Nevertheless I am more deeply impressed as the years pass that the witness of the contemporary liturgical movement is a timely one, that it represents one aspect of the religious revival of our time, and that it may yet prove to be an important if not indispensable element in the world's Christian recovery. There are of course dangers, as well as promise of good, in every movement of God's Holy Spirit within the human spirit; and it is surely providential that the revival of concern about worship has been moving, in Scotland and elsewhere, parallel to the other vital movements of Biblical theology and parochial mission, and at many points in close association with them. Only so can the liturgical movement be saved from becoming ' archaist ', be kept true to the evangelical gospel, and remain livingly contemporary.

It is thus especially appropriate that preaching be considered afresh from the viewpoint of its association with the Church's common prayer. These are different aspects of the divine-human encounter, closely related modes of man's exposure to the eternal Word. It is under the control of this thought of encounter that I am constrained to deal with the integral relationship between the sermon and the rest of the Church's service of worship.

It would be unfitting for lectures on a foundation such as this to represent any particular school of theology or of Biblical interpretation. The present chapters, so far as these questions are concerned, will not, it is hoped, assume anything that is not matter of fairly general agreement among Biblical scholars. What is here debated is not this or that question of scholarship but the application of the results of scholarship in preaching.

One word may be added. It might be thought that in the following pages there is too unquestioning an acceptance of traditional forms, and that what is required now is the minting of a new religious currency. 'It may be', writes L. T. C. Rolt, 'that not only art but religion, in the ritualistic sense, must die before it can be born again; that only after the re-adoption of an organic life out of dire necessity shall we recover that sense of wonder and humility without which neither can flourish.'[1] Undoubtedly there is a serious question here.

Two things may be said about this. First of all, it is everywhere being proved not only that the traditional patterns can be developed as a living apparatus of worship today, but that they cannot in fact be dispensed with, since they embody the tested logic of worship.

Also it is probably true that in the heavily secularized West we are now generally *past* the stage at which traditional forms no longer seem to men to have validity; and that, handled with contemporary realism and spiritual imagination, they come fresh to people who have been born into homes already two or three generations removed from vital churchmanship. Significant of this is the story of the girl, in a new housing area, who apologized to her minister for her parents' absence from church because, she said, ' you see, they are so old-fashioned! '

In an age of multiplied idolatries, superstitions, and illusions the impact of truth may yet be startling. As awakening as the sound of a clarion may one day be that bidding which says: ' Let us worship God ' and ' Hear the Word of God.'

[1] *High Horse Riderless* (London, 1947), ch. iv. p. 163.

# CONTENTS

Chapter Four. THE SONG

Chapter Five. THE MOUTH-PIECE

# CHAPTER ONE

# THE VAGRANT WORD

---

'Even the temple was not represented to the Jews as confining the presence of God within its walls, but was meant to train them to contemplate the image of the true temple.'

CALVIN, *Institutes of the Christian Religion*,
Bk. III, ch. xx. 30-32

'Brethren, pray for us, that the word of the Lord may have free course, and be glorified . . .'

*2 Thessalonians* iii. 1

'He that observeth the wind shall not sow.'

*Ecclesiastes* xi. 4

## 1. 'HEAR THE WORD OF GOD'

In the living thought of the Church the action of preaching is clearly understood to involve an encounter with God. That it is this, and not merely the transmission of a deposit of ideas, is shown by the form of the solemn bidding which introduces lections and sermon in the service of the Reformed Churches. The bidding is: 'Hear the Word of God.' Not 'read it' but 'hear it!'

This bidding means exactly what it says. It is not a pious adjuration from a man at the lectern to men and women in the pew, backed by no sanction but the preacher's earnestness. Still less should it be the almost apologetic, 'Let us read together the Word of God', which bespeaks neither a proper awareness of authority nor a well-considered theology of the Word. The authentic bidding is a command, and as such it should be given. If the minister prefers to regard it as a gracious invitation, it still has all the force of a royal invitation. We are bidden to the awesome privilege of an audience.

In every sense the bidding is imperative. It is imperative in grammar, and in that form it ought to be uttered in church—'Hear the Word of God', for this is a divine command. And it is imperative that it should be heard.

It is imperative not—as has been iterated from the pulpits of the industrialized West so frequently and so un-Biblically during the years of agony—because it is only when men accept Christianity that there can be peace, a peace that is presumably regarded as desirable in order that men, set free from the anxieties attendant upon the 'crash of empires and the war of worlds', may then be able to pursue their private concerns, God or no God. For this will not do. 'Christ', said Kagawa, 'did not die on the cross to propagate humanism.' Nor indeed does humanism become any more a gospel because, in a masked form, it is preached from a Christian pulpit, baptized so to speak with a sprinkling of holy words. This is not what the minister is in the pulpit to preach.

A famous Everest climber, asked why anyone should want to climb the mountain, is reported to have said: 'Because it is there!' And this is why we preach God in Jesus Christ, because, quite simply, God is there, the ultimate and all-interpreting fact. No one can even begin to live—in a way to be called life—who does not with some degree of vision understand the ultimate structure of life and come to terms with it. This must be the foundation of any preaching in which will be heard the ring of authority and the note of hope, simply that it witnesses to facts solid, objective, and ultimate.

It is at this point that the individual must determine also his attitude towards the Church. For the Church is either a human institution, humanly conceived and recruited, exercising useful psychological functions; or it is God's plenipotentiary, like Jeremiah, commanding men to listen:

O earth, earth, earth, hear the word of the Lord!

This is the issue in our time: that in church and outside of it men may be enabled to hear the word of God and to hear it, not as a rarefied voice in the rarefied air of a misunderstood sacrament, but livingly in the Blessed Sacrament because they are hearing it livingly (to quote Isaiah) in ' the highway of the fuller's field '—that is to say, in the midst of the day's traffic, and the better out there in the highway of business because they are hearing it also in a Sacrament rightly understood and administered. It must again be understood not merely as memorial in a restricted and unbiblical sense (since in the New Testament the ' memorial ' is not a mere mental remembering but a remembering in which the very Presence of Christ becomes actual); nor yet as a mechanical channel of grace; but as eucharist, covenant renewal, and communion. The locus of significance of the Blessed Sacrament is to be found not alone, nor perhaps even primarily, in the substance, but in the action; and that action is God's giving of himself in gracious encounter.

This conception dominates all Reformed worship. In the sermon God is not a subject under discussion; he is the Person who introduces the discussion, addressing us in the concrete terms of his present will for our present and our ultimate situation. ' Hear the Word of God! ' ' Listen hard,' the bidding means, ' at any moment God may address you, in such a way that you experience that leap of imaginative understanding which is belief, that kindling of the will which is Christ's love in you, that obedient sense of belonging which is faith.'

Is it possible for preacher and hearer alike to keep fresh week by week throughout a ministry their awareness of preaching as the locus of this august personal action of God himself? See what in plainest terms it means! ' I am Alpha and Omega, the first and the last. I am he who created all things,' and this God is about to speak! And again: ' They led Jesus out to be crucified . . . and the centurion said,

"Truly this man was the Son of God"', and this God is about to speak! Or again, beyond this world of 'succession' to where, even more nearly, you hear the echoes of eternity: 'I beheld a throne in heaven, and those that were about the throne singing "Holy, holy, holy, Lord God Almighty which was, and is, and is to come"', and this God is about to speak!

If this is true, if our people were taught to believe and did believe that the Word of God means encounter, could they any longer regard the Bible, and the preacher's occasionally lame handling of it, as tedious—or even as merely interesting, much in the way that one might find an article on Brazil interesting even though one were not really interested in Brazil? Or would they not come prepared to find it the most important thing in life, a traffic quite personal and practical, with elements in it which are strange and awesome and yet at the same time intimately familiar, as if it were—as indeed it is—a coming home?

## II. THE RESPONSIBILITY OF THE HEARER

It is important to note that the Bible seems to lay as much stress on the responsibility of the hearer as on that of the preacher. The twentieth century, tortured in its mind by the problem of faith on the part of the man in the street and by the all-engrossing problem of communication on the part of the Church, has everywhere insisted on the responsibility of the *preacher*. It is held to be the preacher's business to make himself understood—'please talk our language'—and what is usually intended is that he will talk not merely a language but a content of thought that is congenial to the listener. If this is not forthcoming, the listener (employing a familiar escape-route) holds himself free to contract out of the colloquy.

But God does not hold him free. Throughout its entire

length the Bible insists on the responsibility, not only of the preacher, but of the *hearer*.

There is room for pulpit teaching on this theme. A congregation requires to face the fact that, as a preacher once put it, 'while it is true that the pulpit can cast a blight on the pew, it is also true that the pew can cast a blight on the pulpit.' There are not only different qualities of preacher but different qualities of *hearer*. 'The people said that it thundered! others said, An angel spoke . . .' (John xii. 29).

Why is one person never free from the sense that all life is the occasion of a divine-human colloquy while another apparently is innocent of this awareness? 'How is it', Judas (not Iscariot) asked of Jesus, 'that thou wilt manifest thyself to us and not unto the world?' (The title of the sermon on this text might well be 'Why some people disbelieve'.) Just as you or I might have observed chemical material undergoing tests and noticed nothing significant, while a Rutherford, seeing the same thing, would be thrillingly aware of the unveiling of 'things kept secret from the foundation of the world'; or as Constable the painter might have looked at three trees in a field and seen in them a picture while 'the cow in the meadow sees the same thing and makes nothing of it', so it seems possible for people to be cows in the matter of faith, unaware of being touched by God at a hundred points every day.

No one will question that this is part of the preacher's problem today. The real ages of great preaching have always been the ages of great hearing. It is not possible to say that great preaching is prior to great hearing or vice versa, but only that they closely condition each other.

Certainly the conditions of life today, ranging from the absence of intellectual demand in screen entertainment to the overcrowded nature of many people's personal programme, militate against deep inward hearing of the Word from the Unseen. If prayer is 'punctuated silence', then hurry makes prayer impossible by eliminating one of its conditions. Preoccupation, quite as much as sin, is the enemy of devotion. 'How much', cried Joseph Parker, 'we expect of the poor man who leads our worship and directs our studies: what little pity we have for him. Every Sabbath he must perform a miracle of resurrection upon our dead piety; we have been in the world six days, buying, selling, getting gain, or making losses, we have forgotten the whole conception of God, and we expect some brother man to come and revive us and recreate us . . .'[1]

## III. THE WORD AS PERSONAL

Nevertheless his people's very slowness to hear is also part of the preacher's responsibility and defines some part of his programme. If there is widespread misunderstanding in the pew as to what the phrase ' the Word of God ' means, there is place for pulpit teaching here also. The Word of God is not simply the Bible or the sermon regarded as a written or spoken account of God's will for past ages or even for our day. The ' Word of God ' is personal. It is *whatever God may say to men* through the Bible and sermon, or even without Bible and sermon; and at any moment he may be saying to two different people in the same congregation by means of the same Scripture two quite separate things, matched to the needs and capacities of each. The word of the preacher is no more than the locus of encounter. The sermon is the thing outwardly spoken; the Word of God is the thing inwardly heard. It is possible to hear the sermon and not to hear the Word of God.

Consider how this personal or dynamic conception of the Word may help modern people in their reading of the Bible. It is not difficult to understand the reaction of a thoughtful but uninstructed hearer of the 109th Psalm—that apparently

[1] *City Temple Sermons* (London, 1902), Vol. vi, p. 70.

venomous prayer of a man concerning his enemy: 'Let his days be few; and let another take his office. Let his children be fatherless, and his wife a widow . . .' It would not be surprising if such a hearer, conscious of a deep sense of moral outrage, should almost inevitably end by asking the wrong questions and arriving at the wrong answers about the inspiration of the Bible.

What is a preacher to say about such a scripture? The problem is not really solved by the explanation that the maledictory psalms are instances of primitive medicine or exorcism of evil spirits from a community, true as these explanations may be as far as they go. On the other hand you do offer the essential and positive answer when you bid the hearer to 'hear the Word of God' even at so disturbing a place in Holy Scripture. Hearing, in this attitude of listening, the hideous proposal of the psalm, may there not flash across the hearer's mind the recollection of our Lord's utterance upon the cross: 'Father, forgive them, for they know not what they do'? and in contrasting the two scriptures the psalm may become a mirror in which God shows him his own heart—'This, in the psalm, was you yesterday or last week.' In that instant he has heard the Word of God even through the vehicle of a psalm of malediction. This is what one may call the dynamic—better call it the Biblical or personal—conception of the Word of God.

St. Paul, facing the challenge of a missionary ministry, asked: 'How shall they hear without a preacher?' It is also possible to ask: 'How can they preach without a hearer?' Again and again preachers, hard put to it because of some contemporary famine of *hearing* the Word, have asked precisely this. Is it possible to preach in genuine confidence of a hearing today—when some churches seem to have given up the attempt and are substituting instead a humanly contrived *mystique* for the authentic mystery—the disclosed secret—of the Gospel? The answer can be expressed in our Lord's own words: 'My time is not yet come: but your time is always ready.'

The preacher must go on working. He is a prophet, not a crystal-gazer, thus he is not susceptible to discouragement in the last resort. He requires to remind himself that the contemporary situation is never one in which elements of faith are being added to society's stock of faith or subtracted from it, in such a way that one can visualize the imminent extinction of faith or, if the balance be a credit one, a religious revival. The situation is always dynamic because of the nature of men and the fact of grace. The Church is always—at every moment of history—dying and being reborn. In the souls of men faith is perennially suffering assault and being revitalized. This is actually the Christian's own daily experience as it is the world's experience. The situation is never static but always dynamic because, whether men realize it or not, God is incessantly active.

In this, as in other things, we are apt to have from God exactly what we ask of him. The preacher must believe that at any moment of the human utterance God may send the Holy Spirit to witness, in the heart of some hearer, that what the preacher is proclaiming from the Bible is the eternal truth of God and his contemporary Word. The believing preacher will discover good reason to believe. There is a kind of pragmatism in this traffic of man with God which is soundly Biblical.

Humanly viewed there is a dilemma in preaching. It was because he resolutely faced the full implications of this dilemma that St. Paul came to see, as otherwise he could not, the divine action breaking into the circle of necessity, and to cast himself, as otherwise he could never have done, upon the *grace* of God:

'You say Israel is to call on the Name of the Lord, but how are they to call on him in whom they have not believed? . . . You say they haven't heeded the Gospel?

True. That is because they don't have faith, and unfaith is deaf. And yet faith comes by what is heard '—once more the personal Word!—' and what is heard comes by preaching of Christ . . .' The situation is rather like that of a man looking for his glasses but unable to find them because he does not have his glasses on.

It is a dilemma of human logic. In fact, however, it is the place of God's action—if grace is indeed God's breaking through the circle of logical necessity so as to make actual what, humanly speaking, was not possible. In practice, this is the true reading of the human situation, that it is always hopeful because of grace. Therefore Paul argues, in what would be a classic *non sequitur* apart from the fact of grace : ' But I ask, have they not heard? Indeed they have . . .'

Every preacher with long experience discovers this to be true. There are listeners who ' hear ' more than they are prepared to admit. Or, perhaps more accurately, they know themselves to be so near to ' hearing ' that, in the Biblical image, they quickly ' stop their ears '. To be within range of hearing is disturbing. To hear and admit hearing is catastrophic. Some deafness is really an unwillingness to be disturbed.

Also, as the Reformed Churches ought not to be in danger of forgetting, it is where the Bible is opened in the midst of the church that the Voice is most likely to be heard.

The Bible is the book of a Voice, not merely of a message. It begins with the Voice in the Garden and ends with ' the Spirit and the Bride ' saying ' Come! ' This ' Word of God ' is something more than a speech-symbol indicating meaning. It is a creative Word which effects something. Men hear it, and whether they accept or reject it they are never the same again. Even when the ears are ' stopped ', the corridors of the mind are full of echoes. It is in this confidence that we preach.

## IV. HISTORIC PARALLELS

Once more it is this fact of sovereign grace that controls all Christian understanding of history.

It is relatively easy to systematize the facts of history so as to discover in them grounds for hope that good may triumph; but it is a precarious if not dishonest enterprise. The witness of history, after all, proclaims that we justifiably preach in hope, not because history's pages are blazoned with the triumphs of the Church (there have, after all, been other and very different triumphs), and certainly not because the historical actuary can balance cheering factors against discouraging ones and strike a credit balance, but simply because the Church's triumphs and other triumphs alike have taken place in a world created and ruled by a gracious God. This fact sets Pilate in perspective and Christ also, Christ gloriously and Pilate as under judgement and ultimately doomed.

It does indeed appear at first glance as if the Church has always, at climacteric periods, seen herself confronted with the threat of extinction; while looking back, we can now read in the situation pregnant opportunities. Though Paul in his faith wrote: 'A great door and effectual is opened unto me and there are many adversaries . . .' (a text this for a sermon on 'disguised opportunities'), it must have appeared to less trusting men, to Demas for instance, that the adversaries were in process of out-staring the Christian opportunists. The primitive Church was propagating what to the Jews was a blasphemous heresy, to the pagans an atheistic impiety (since, lacking images, it appeared to have no god), and to the Romans what could readily be interpreted as the sinister programme of an underground movement. In retrospect we know enough about the inwardness of that ancient classical world to hear, as muted counterpoint to the marching of confident legions, the 'pattering feet of the dogs of fate.' We can understand how, after the fierce hostility to Christ was overcome, the faith appeared as a fresh and inviting thing in that faded world; and that God was able to use (after all it was his own creation) the new moral, spiritual, and intellectual factors in the lives of the Christians to work a miracle of grace.

Men do not customarily read their own times wisely. It is humanly remarkable that Paul *at the time* should have discerned so surely that it was the ' fulness of the time '.

The New Testament makes the reason clear. He discerned the historic opportunity because he first had a vivid sense of what was expressed by the word *kairos*—the God-ordained season. If it were God's chosen time, the apostle's work would not be a matter of shame. And so it proved.

Later, it must have seemed as if the post-Constantine Church, at the time of the barbarian invasions, was presented with a threat of extinction which we now see to have been a disguised opportunity. The Faith actually appealed, but now on quite different grounds, to the northern peoples. When the barbarian invaders broke through and settled in the lands of the Roman Empire, Christianity confronted them, as Herbert Butterfield expressed it, ' as part of a superior culture which they envied and desired to appropriate for themselves '.[1] Today, it is affirmed, the Faith is associated in the popular mind with a type of culture, a social and moral economy, which are in part discredited, in part despised, and are certainly to a large extent rejected of men. In terms of its own crude jargon the Western world has had Christianity, while the resurgent East still to some extent associates it with (from its viewpoint) a tarnished imperialism. This makes for an atmosphere not so much hostile as indifferent.

During a later and equally crucial century, it seemed that

[1] Butterfield goes on to point out that there is a parallel between that earlier Christianity and modern Communism at least in the order of events: the going out of the first missionaries, the planting of cells of believers, the conversion of strategically-placed individuals and groups, the capture of government, mass conversion followed by propaganda, various disciplines, and the heresy-hunt. *Christianity in European History* (London, 1952), ch. II, pp. 22 f.

once again the bark of the Church was threatened with ship-
wreck, while we can now see that the winds of opportunity
were actually in her sails. 'New signs of misfortune', wrote
Calvin, 'are visible in every direction as we look around us,
so that the future seems to hold nothing except the complete
downfall of the Church. But one thought, none the less,
uplifts my heart and gives me new courage. I say to myself:
Since God has begun this wonderful reformation of his
Church, he never meant to awaken empty hopes, which
would soon be swept away.' (This passage was quoted in a
German pamphlet by Dr. Martin Niemöller during the early
period of Nazi rule.)

In retrospect we can see, more clearly than was possible
for the men of the sixteenth century, that it was with a
different, but still potent appeal, that the Reformed preaching commended itself to the men of that age. It is normally
unsafe to generalize about a period. We know enough however about the sixteenth century to be able to say that the
Reformation was not a primary social cause but was, in some
of its elements, a religious effect. On the human side it was
the upshot, in the field of religion, of forces which were
already creating the beginnings of democracy in politics, of
freedom in commerce, and of independence (that is to say,
willingness to open the mind to facts) in the realm of intellectual thought. To that extent it carried men with it because
in some degree it chimed with what many were then feeling.
In a word, it rang a bell.[1]

---

[1] The parallel extends further. In England, as the Puritan temper
of the seventeenth century sobered the colour of men's thoughts, once
more that attitude reflected a current mood of general insecurity
strongly contrasted with the bold and colourful originality of the
Elizabethans. 'The congregations', wrote the late Lord Tweedsmuir,
'which listened to Donne's analysis of sin and his pictures of the
"various and vagabond heart of the sinner" thronged to St. Paul's
because the preacher was in tune with their own thoughts.' *Montrose*
(Edinburgh, 1928), Introduction.

It might seem, however, that today the Church, so far from expressing in religious terms a current mood, must preach a gospel which affronts every presupposition of the modern mind. (The truth and qualifications of this statement we must consider in a later chapter.)

Are such analyses really valid for us? Is it true to say that formerly the Church always found herself in a favourable strategic position but that she no longer does so, because now the Gospel enjoys none of the advantages of the earlier opportunities—the charm of novelty, the prestige of association with a valued culture, let alone any kind of consonance with the dominant moods, aims, or thoughts of modern men? Is this indeed so?

## V. CONTEMPORARY OCCASIONS OF DIFFICULTY

That there are present-day occasions of difficulty in presenting the Gospel is very evident. Every period of history throws up its particular heresies of belief or of temper which aggravate the difficulty of winning a hearing for the Gospel. Their form is transient; the substance is perennial, since it will usually be found that what underlies them proves to be the ancient stubborn evasions and revolts against God of which the Bible itself is the classical text-book. This means incidentally that if you preach faithfully from the Bible, you preach directly to the times you live in.

So far from being discouraging, then, this fact of difficulty is the very reason for our ministry and indicates some part of our preaching programme.

A fascinating passage in St. Paul's letter to Titus might well serve as the appointed lesson for all times of momentary discouragement (there is also a sermon in it for the encouragement of a congregation in its parochial responsibility). You do not catch the significance of the passage fully unless you try to imagine the letter to which it is clearly an answer. There

are sermons that sound more like the bleat of the lost sheep
than the confident call of the Good Shepherd, and it may be
that Titus's letter was of that type. Pondering Paul's reply,
one wonders if Titus had written something like this:

Dear Paul,
    Why did God send me here to Crete?
    This is not a ' desirable parish '. It would take years and years
of sweated labour—and you know very well the Church is not
a good employer—to make anything of the place. The Cretans
are a miserable lot, cheats, liars, drunken, and pretty foul-
mouthed. . .

We can only guess at the contents of Titus's letter. We do
have Paul's reply. Paul says in effect:

Dear Titus—my true son in the faith, you ask why you are
posted to Crete? Because there is so much wrong in Crete that
needs to be put right! Yes, everybody knows about the Cretans
—they are a byword for every kind of vice. What you say is all
too true. But *that's why you are there*—to show them the kind
of character Christ creates through faith in Him . . .

In imagination one stands in the room with Titus as he
receives the letter, picturing the expression on the young
man's face as he reads. It is not difficult to imagine him,
braced and even deeply thrilled as he sees things in a new
and splendid light. Now he prays, giving himself to Christ
again, and giving himself to that parish in a fresh and decisive
commitment; for in every ministry that is to be worth while
something of the patience of Christ's redemptive passion
must be reproduced afresh.

' Difficulties in Crete ' have been a familiar theme of
reports to Church courts in our time. ' Difficulties in Crete,'
reports Titus. ' That's why you are there! ' is Christ's reply.
    This means in practice that it is precisely at such places of
stubborn resistance to the Gospel, whether the resistance is
of the will or of the understanding, that our preaching comes

to life. If it does not come to life, it may be for one or other of two reasons.

Freya Stark describes how during the First World War the town of Lowestoft was shelled but little damage was done. ' A shell ran alongside one street through the top floor of one house (and the inhabitants were in the kitchen), then through the bottom story of the next (and the inhabitants were on the landing above), and finally settled, unexploded, somewhere in the third.

'Most of the shells did not explode because, being meant to impact against the hard steel of battleships, the walls of Lowestoft houses were too *soft* for them.'[1]

Some sermons fail to register because the modern mind is theologically so woolly that there is nothing for the Gospel to bite on. Professor T. E. Jessop, from wide experience of speaking to men in the forces during the war, testified that great numbers of them could not get hold of abstract ideas: ' It is not that they won't; it is that they can't.'[2] (To this difficulty also we return in a later chapter.)

It is likewise possible, when preaching has proved ineffective, that it has itself lacked the 'bite' of relevancy, the cutting edge of the scalpel; and it is for this reason and not on grounds of scholarship that some sermons are a disappointment. The sermon begins with a sound and quite interesting exegesis which enables one to understand why certain words were written in the eighth century before Christ. But the preacher has not yet *preached*. The true preacher makes one aware—excitingly, uncomfortably, gratefully aware—that the God who busied himself with Moses or Rehoboam in ancient times is speaking at that moment in that church in contemporary idiom to oneself.

God, after all, does not speak in a void. Like an accom-

[1] *Beyond Euphrates* (London, 1951), p. 56.
[2] *Vide* Anglican report, *Towards the Conversion of England* (London, 1945).

plished speaker in any company, God speaks always to the
occasion. Without the occasion there is no speech. Ideas, as
Thomas Mann said, do not live if they do not have to fight.
It is the same with the Gospel. The Gospel must have something to bite on, and we ought to see that it does.


VI. THE CONTEMPORARY BIBLE

The preacher requires to remember that while he is—in
every generation—facing a new situation, he is not facing a
new predicament. The essential human predicament remains
the same. And if it is at the point of incidence of contemporary stresses that we make our difficult witness, it is by
virtue of the extraordinary opportunities which these difficulties actually present to us that we are able to preach in hope
and more than sober confidence.

The great preachers have always known this. Read Hugh
Latimer, Bishop of Worcester, one of the greatest popular
preachers the Anglican Church has known, who as a young
man in 1524 first began under Reforming influences to
'smell the word of God' (the phrase is his).

Living in a century of extraordinary happenings, he
preached from the Bible and to the occasion. Very charm-
ingly, in preaching before the clergy, he warned them
against thinking that 'God walked up and down in heaven,
and thinketh never a deal of our affairs. But, my good
brethren, err not so; stick not you to such your imaginations.
For if ye inwardly behold these words',—the words of his
text—'if ye diligently roll them in your minds, and after
explicate and open them, ye shall see our time much touched
in these mysteries. Ye shall perceive that God by this example shaketh us by the noses and pulleth us by the ears . . .'[1]

[1] Sermon preached the 9th day of June, the twenty-eighth year of
the reign of King Henry VIII on Luke xvi, 'the children of this
world, etc.'.

Again, after listening to murmurs from certain quarters about the dissolution of the monasteries, Latimer used the occasion to preach a Biblical doctrine of the Church. 'It is a common speech amongst the people, and much used, that they say, "All religious houses are pulled down: " which is a very peevish thing, and not true, for they are not pulled down. That man and that woman that live together godly and quietly, doing the works of their vocation, and fear God, hear his word and keep it; that same is a religious house, that is, that house that pleaseth God . . .'[1]

Surely the Word of God that was vagrant in Galilee and Jerusalem, in Antioch and Asia, and in Latimer's time, is vagrant still, to be heard by those who have ears amid the conditions of modern life.

In each of these conditions there is a will of God to be discerned, spoken, and heard, in judgement or correction, in approval or for 'strengthening the things that remain'. A popular preacher of a former generation, on being asked how he did it, moved one finger slightly up the other and said, 'you must tell the people so much but not *so much!*'—in other words, don't strain them beyond a certain point. In our Lord's day the popular synagogue preacher was expected to have an attractive physical presence, and his words—'like those of the bride to the bridegroom', 'sweet as honey'— were expected to be conciliatory and not too personal.[2] One scents an element of deceit in this.

Now it is true that the Church, while not sounding like a benevolent uncle, ought not to sound like a testy schoolmaster, always and only finding fault with 'this perverse generation'. Certainly our Lord spoke passages of sternest judgement; yet one remembers when his heart overflowed in gracious and grateful approval. Why not a contemporary

[1] Fifth sermon on the Lord's Prayer.
[2] Alfred Edersheim, *Life and Times of Jesus the Messiah* (London, 1886), Vol. 1, ch. x, p. 477.

sermon on 'the things Christ approves'? It is not difficult to
find Scripture for it: 'Blessed art thou, Simon bar-Jona, for
flesh and blood hath not revealed it unto thee, but . . .' Or
another on 'Christ and our modern achievements' from the
passage: 'I am not come to destroy, but to fulfil'? After
all our Lord, when he spoke these words about the Old
Covenant, used them in explicit reference to the whole of the
covenant culture of his time. If the Old Covenant and its
related culture required to be fulfilled in Christ, so do the
latent and germinal virtues in the modern character and way
of life. At many points, even in 'this perverse generation',
Christ must surely say: 'There is good in this; I am not
come to destroy but to fulfil it.' Whether it be the extraordinary, perilous gift of God through the scientific discovery
of things kept hidden from the foundation of the world; or
the huge new experiments in social planning and government of societies—'I am not come to destroy but to fulfil all
these things!'

There surely you have the nub of much of the truth about
human lives and human societies. They achieve much, but
for a variety of reasons they stop short of richer fulfilment.

Hence the sting and edge of the challenge may be illustrated by King Ahab's charge to his men: 'Know ye that
Ramoth in Gilead is ours, and we be still, and take it not out
of the hand of the king of Syria?' (I Kings xxii. 3.) Israel's
soil was regarded as holy and inalienable, yet the campaign
of recovery had not been pushed to the limit. Ramoth-Gilead
remained in Syrian keeping. Unfortunately Ahab's spirit
awoke too late. He had already made a treaty, an inadequate
treaty after a successful war. But he was right in his dis-
content. Earlier, at the crucial point of the campaign before
the treaty was made, he ought to have sounded that rallying-
cry: 'Know ye that Ramoth in Gilead is ours, and we be
still, and take it not out of the hand of the king of Syria?'

Is it not a vivid picture of things, an analogy of much that

we see around us? Are there not territories as yet unclaimed
—they belong by right to Christ—in the lives of men where
some flaw of character, some defect of resolve, some fatal
indecision supervenes between early idealisms and their fulfilment: in the Church that rests content with the forms of
godliness, the ceremonial of the cult, but stops short of the
redemptive concern involved in being the *Body* of Christ, so
that ' the regions beyond ', that are to be found even in one's
own parish, are left unclaimed for Christ: in the individual
religious life, where piety may successfully mask an unwillingness to train for the tasks of the Kingdom in up-to-date
modes of Christian accomplishment—in techniques for example of Christian education, mission, and corporate prayer:
and not least in our public life where so much that is a matter
of thankfulness to God has come about in our time, where
nevertheless legislation lays down the minimum duty that is
required of men and Trade Unions lay down the maximum
that is permitted, and thus a norm is established, not only in
industry (where sociologically it is explicable) but throughout
the ranges of social life? And men are content to have it so.
Thus at many points love stops short of her fulfilment, which
is always a stooping and washing of another's feet. It is possible to be too easily content even with apparently great
achievement. And this word too must be preached so as to
be heard in our streets—this vagrant Word.

Or think of the moral and spiritual damage done in our
time by the power of uncriticized assumptions. The influences
that play upon all of us today, even the most wary of us,
resemble the force of wind and water upon a ship at sea. Of
these the currents are the more subtly perilous. The force of
the winds is warningly palpable, that of the current more
insidious. The wind blusters. It proclaims: ' I am determined, if I can, to carry you in my direction.' The current
silently does so, in its own direction.

There are influences of that kind today. Plain invitations

to vice or error are recognized for what they are. The Devil's deadliest weapons are the uncriticized assumptions that are started in society, many if not most of them commercially inspired for gain. Years ago Miss Dorothy Sayers expressed her profound disquiet about the personal angle from which everything was being viewed: 'This irrational obsession', she wrote, 'pervades the newspapers, makes the lives of public characters a burden to them, distracts public worship from its proper object, and is rapidly destroying the intelligence of the people. It is as though nobody cared for what is said, but only for who says it.'

Since these words were written affairs have moved much further in this direction. There are, as in the past, those who realize that money can be made by exploiting human passions, hence the insistent exploitation of the twin themes of wealth and sex. In some journals the minx and the millionaire monopolize the headlines and main pages, their worthless stories cunningly disguised as objective news. They are, in fact, nothing of the sort. They are simply the shrewdest of 'sales-lines'.

The preacher who needs a text which allows the word of God to be heard in respect of this morbid condition of society may well find it in the story of Absalom's flight from his royal father's army, one verse of which records this vivid detail—during the course of the flight 'the wood devoured more people that day than the sword devoured' (2 Sam. xviii. 8). In its own fashion this describes the way in which many people are entrapped by false values almost unawares. Far fewer people are, so to speak, *slain* morally than are *enmeshed*. The sword stands, symbolically, for the obvious spiritual perils, the invitations which are plainly recognized as Devil's lures. The wood stands for life's entanglements. It expresses the way in which people, by reason of their associations and the assumptions of the circle they move in, unwittingly accept second-rate standards and false philosophies. It is the peril of uncriticized assumptions.

Yet there are some who are beginning to be unhappy about this situation, and long to hear the voice of reality. In the churches, on any Sunday, most people, since their previous appearance at worship, have been continually played upon by the spiritually chilling air of a world that is competitive commercially and socially. They come, prayerless in the main, having lived six days on the assumption that the things which count are the things that can be counted. Yet there is a reserve in their worldly commitment. Some, perhaps more than one would think, are conscious, even between Sundays, of an uneasy feeling of betrayal—the condition P. T. Forsyth defined as 'conscious self-seeking more or less in protest against itself'.

Or contrast the witness of the Bible with the prevailing attitudes of the characteristic man in the world of welfare states. The Bible is class-conscious from end to end. We may feel disturbed by this fact; and indeed the dislike of it has been responsible for a certain watering down of the Gospel and for some consequent spiritual debility.

Nevertheless the fact is there. The Bible divides people into classes. You cannot read in St. John, on the theme of the Good Shepherd, without being aware of Christ's judgement, perennially applied to society, in the picture of the three classes into which men are divided. Here is the robber class, predatory in the sense of being resolved to *get* as much as possible out of life with no determination to give in return—'If people are mugs' (a shrug here) it's their pigeon! ' Here too is the hireling class who know their hours and their contract to a second and a halfpenny and will do nothing except what they are paid for. And here, in startling challenge and appeal, is the Good Shepherd who gives without stint with love's giving.

Moreover all these are themes that demand to be treated *theologically*. Merely to fill in the blank spaces in the sheets

of sermon paper with conventional strictures on the supposed
'materialism' of our time, without theological interpretation,
is not preaching the Gospel, and may even so falsify the
terms of the Gospel as to add to the spiritual confusion of
the listener.

What does the Christian preacher in fact mean by the peril
of materialism? If he fears a selfish and hazardous use of the
marvellous material resources of the world, it is legitimate
to say so. He requires, however, to insist that such resources
are a gift of God's providence, and all God's gifts are perilous.
The Church, then, dares not merely criticize 'materialism'
without definition. The Church exists to assert the material.
The Gospel is the ground of a theology that is creational and
incarnational. In Holy Baptism and in the Eucharist the
material becomes sacramental. This could not be true of the
sacraments without being true of the whole world of matter.
There is a sense in which, to the Christian, the universe itself
is sacramental. The sacramental understanding is the living
theme in those most materialistic of New Testament writings, St. John's Gospel and Epistles, which deal throughout
with that 'which we have heard, which we have seen with
our eyes, which we have looked upon, and our hands have
handled, of the Word of life' (1 John i. 1).

This understanding seems to be common to the liturgical
movement and those movements which are aware of the
social implications of Christian faith. Since our people are
fated to come to terms with 'the material' in the difficult
ways of the world, our preaching must not fail to reveal
*matter* as the vehicle of the holy. If we ignore the material
or treat it as evil or indifferent, we automatically 'deliver it
over to the Devil'.

To some extent it may be due to past failure in sacramental
understanding that this has in fact been happening on a
widespread scale today. Liturgical (including as it does
sacramental) teaching is closely relevant to our need. St.

John refers to what happens when the material world is viewed and interpreted apart from God. There is a threefold outcome: 'the lust of the flesh'—that is to say pleasure without responsibility, natural passion without ultimate caring; 'the lust of the eyes'—that is, the way natural passion sees, without reverence; and the 'pride' or vainglory of life—which is the determination to be one's own God.

It is unfortunate that the terms 'puritan' and 'catholic' should have been so abused as now to be set over against each other, as if 'puritan' implied negative morality and subjective-individualist worship, and 'catholic' the positive in conduct, and in worship the objective-corporate. Nothing is easier than to talk of puritan cant, but the gibe cuts both ways. 'Never forget', warned Joseph Parker, 'the cant that is talked against cant.'

In this age of ecumenical ferment, the preacher, especially if he be also the liturgical arbiter, requires to be very clear in his mind as to the significance of such terms as puritan and catholic before he commits himself to the undefined use of them. For while there is a primitive historic catholicism which is essentially sacramental and which is the tradition of the Reformed, as it is of the Anglican Churches, there is always, bidding for a vote, a fashionable 'catholicism' which is a ready way of evading the elements of austerity in the Gospel.

There is a discerning passage in George Fox's Journal in which he describes a visit to the house of one John Audland:

. . . and there came John Story to me and lighted his pipe of tobacco. And said he, 'Will you take a pipe of tobacco?' saying, 'Come; all is ours'. And I looked upon him to be a forward bold lad; and tobacco I did not take, but it came into my mind that the lad might think I had not unity with the creation. For I saw he had a flashy empty notion of religion. So I took his pipe and put it to my mouth, and gave it to him again to stop him lest his rude tongue should say I had not unity with the creation.

John Story was wrong, but John Story could have been right, on very similar terms. For there is a deep and a shallow way of saying the same thing. At the deeper level the true catholicism, which is material and sacramental, and the true puritanism, which is a protest and an appeal for reverent use, are one. They are both expressed, in perfect harmony, in a sermon by a prince of medieval preachers, Eckhart: ' To it ' (that is, the soul) 'all creatures are pure to enjoy; for it enjoyeth all creatures in God and God in all creatures.'

This issue, embracing as it does some of the thorniest problems of the twentieth century, in the fields of personal and public ethics, will not be solved except there be radical clarification of the doctrinal understanding. It is the handling of the exciting substance of life, so perilous yet designed to have sacramental significance, that will identify the Christian interpretation of nature and of culture, which is man's ingenious structure upon nature. It is here too that the Bible, rightly interpreted, will prove to be the locus of the living Word of God to this generation, speaking always to man's condition.

VII. THEOLOGICAL AND MORAL CLARIFICATIONS

It is, however, within this region of Biblical interpretation and theological understanding (closely connected as these are) that the preacher comes up against a soft hedge of religious confusion or a hard wall of religious refusal. Some of the occasions of refusal are not irremovable, given a preacher who has himself experienced existential tension by discovering along the whole range of his religious thinking that the smooth clichés whether of Edwardian optimism (which managed to remain unaware of the tragic elements inherent in history) or of the contemporary tranquillizer religion (which is a not infrequent reaction to those tragic elements), are mocked out of court by that most effective of advocates, harsh reality. Such preachers may not at first catch the ear of a generation. They may at first require to do something more important, catch the ear of the serious and creative minority. However sensitive and critically aware the preaching, the hearer whose outlook is conditioned by current assumptions remains very stubborn. Yet none is finally insusceptible to the inbreak of God's personal word.

Nevertheless it is the preacher's responsibility to understand his auditory if he can, and to know the *malaise* at the heart of modern religious hesitations. Condemnation is not enough.

There is the conditioned unbelief which is due to insistent political propaganda. In this propaganda the human animal's primary interests are defined and represented as economically rooted; while religion is represented as, in one way or another, qualifying these interests adversely. This is only one part, and possibly a passing phase, of a wider and less transient problem, that of the difficulties of faith due to a changing culture. This aspect of the problem of communication was alluded to by an English bishop, who said that, for modern industrial workers, the parable of the man who sowed tares in his neighbour's field would require to be translated as the story of the man who threw the spanner into the works. The problem here however is not the relatively superficial one of discovering words and analogies from familiar current situations. It is an inherent problem because the tendency of a religious cult is to be conservative, while the nature of history is always to be changing. Thus the believer or would-be believer is conscious of a certain unreality when he is asked to express and thereby to profess to feel his religion, the substance of which is unchanging, in *forms* which he regards as period-pieces and not of his own period.

The problem is indeed more stubborn even than this. As we have already noted, a person's outlook may be unwittingly conditioned by the uncriticized assumptions of his generation. This happens—still unwittingly—even to religious people, and it is they who feel the tension of inner dispeace, even when they do not understand its sources. A person is either a wholehearted believer, a wholehearted unbeliever, or, as someone put it, 'a civil war'.

There remains, pervading most other areas of difficulty, the problem posed by the clash of what many believe (often mistakenly) to be the witness of 'science' and what they think is the witness of the Bible. The refusal to believe that the walls of Jericho did actually fall down at the blast of a trumpet may be a refusal which is not so much an actual religious denial as a debate on the threshold of faith.

Such a difficulty is artificial, due to a defective theology of the Word of God itself. 'Kindergarten and backwoods religion', wrote Nels Ferré, 'cannot cope with the growth of modern knowledge.' No, but God can and does. For the Divine Word is simply the Word of the Divine, personal and immediate. And when someone *knows* himself to have met God and to have been dealt with by God, this experience transcends all other difficulties and stamps them as either mistaken or mis-stated. Only one difficulty then remains. It is the difficulty of obedience.

If the experience of faith does not as yet appear to be either widespread or deep, nevertheless there does exist, to a greater degree than at first appears, an awareness of God, even if it is not clearly defined, wherever people find themselves exposed to the Divine Word.

This half-awareness awaits an interpreter. People do have experience of God but do not realize that it is of *God* that they are having experience. This seems to be clear from the fact that frequently their spiritual apprehension rises above its ordinary level in the form of strange oblique confessions of faith or of something which at any moment God may kindle into faith. In its negative form it can be traced as a radical lack of confidence, not, be it well noted, in the claims of religion, but on the contrary in any claim that is not religious. Karl Heim describes how visitors to the Krupps works used to be shown a steam hammer, which, when the operator pressed a knob, came down with force guaranteed to flatten anything. The controlling mechanism however was adjusted to a hairsbreadth accuracy so that a wrist-watch could be placed beneath it and, if you chose, the hammer would stop falling exactly before striking it. Yet, whenever the engineer invited anyone to place his hand beneath the hammer, no one took up the challenge. This attitude extends far beyond the field of modern mechanics. Its significance for faith is like the significance in astronomy of the dark side of the moon. In a negative way it hints at an unwillingness to trust anything but God.

More positively and humanly—in the parochial setting—this half-awareness is only lightly masked. It can be discerned beneath the excuses people make about conduct, about their families, even—and this often in surprising quarters—about absence from public worship. An excuse betokens the recognition of a standard; this particular kind of excuse betokens the recognition of a divine standard. The recognition demonstrates itself by many forms of proxy religion which indicate that people are merely postponing a decision in an issue which they acknowledge to be a valid one. We read in the Gospel of the woman of Samaria, with whom Jesus talked by the well, that when she went into the city to find and bring her friends, she 'left her waterpot'—presumably implying that she meant to come back. Is this the explanation of the strange and persistent habit, which even apparently godless parents have, of bringing their children to the font for baptism and afterwards leaving them like spiritual waifs on the church doorstep for admission to Sunday School. They have, so to speak, left their waterpot. They have not finally broken off the encounter. They mean to come back

VIII. THE PREACHER'S PROSPECTUS

It is tempting to attempt a prospectus for Christendom. What in fact does the future hold for the Church? The only Christian answer must be our Lord's, that the secret of the future is not ours but God's, and only 'the unfolding issues of the present' are ours. Nor must we stand in God's way by assuming that God has no new thing to do in the world for individuals, for societies, and for his Church.

Mrs. Roosevelt is reported to have said in a luncheon speech in London, 'At home I try very hard to say that our failures lie in the realm of lack of understanding of the needs, thinking, and longings of the uncommitted peoples.' This is also the position in the field of religion which, after all, is the whole field of life. Great numbers of people, not only in politics but in basic faith, are as yet uncommitted. What the prospectus for Christendom will look like in a hundred years, as to the numbers of Christians, the unity of the Church, or the manner of our worship, who can tell? It is not yet our business to know.

'There shall no sign be given it,' said Jesus, 'but the sign of Jonas the prophet.' Beyond the Resurrection-meaning stamped upon the saying by the evangelist, there are imaginative applications which the preacher may well apply to his own situation. To the preaching minister one meaning suggests itself. The sign that was given *to* Jonah was a sign that could only be wilfully misunderstood: it was the command: 'Go, preach in Nineveh!', and when Jonah hesitated, was repeated without amendment: 'Go, preach in Nineveh!', and when Jonah fled in the opposite direction, not wanting to believe, was simply repeated: 'Go, preach in Nineveh!', until Jonah broke, obeyed, and went.

And the sign that was given to Nineveh was *Jonah*, the strange fact of a man under authority not of this world.

This is the significance of preaching. It is a startling and supernatural thing to be a preacher of the Word. It would indeed be a responsibility so overwhelming as to be insupportable except that he does not stand alone. 'Thou hast a good second', wrote Thomas Boston, the probationer. 'Christ is concerned for his own seed as well as thou.'

And his continuing Passion is fruitful still. The Church has always made her more notable advances in the ages when she has been compelled to live and think, as we would express it today, existentially, when, that is to say, she has not yet become clear as to the final shape of her dogmas, her administration, or her mission, but is living closely under the guidance of the Holy Spirit. One would expect the ages of great preaching to be the ages of spectacular advance, but it does not necessarily happen so. The first classical age of Christian preaching—or at least of the making of great sermons—came in the period of consolidation and deepened comprehension after the Church had subdued the empire of Constantine. By then the Christian thought-forms had been so hammered out as to offer a pliable and ready idiom for the preachers. And they used it to eloquent effect. But this was not, strikingly enough, the significant age of Christian advance. The age of advance was the period in the earlier centuries when the Church's doctrines were not yet finally codified nor her rubrics and liturgies fixed. Her power lay in this, that she was not telling a story of other ages' past encounters with God, but was seen to be a Church whose worship and whose thought alike were, in that very age, the fruit of encounter and the locus of encounter also.

This ought to encourage us. It is in fact our situation today.

Such a Church all men can understand because she is herself a witness transcending language. She is seen also to be the locus of God's encounter with contemporary men. Without that experience of living encounter there is no authority either in the preaching or the preacher.

# CHAPTER TWO

# THE LITURGY

---

' Now may Israel say:
    If it had not been the Lord who was on our side . . .
then the waters had overwhelmed us, the stream had gone
over our soul; then the proud waters had gone over our
soul . . .'

*Rubric and prayer in Psalm* cxxiv.

' Let all the people say, Amen.'

*Rubric at end of Psalm* cvi.

## 1. A PATTERN OF PRAYER AND PREACHING

We turn now to consider the relationship of the Word of
God to the liturgy, and more especially what may be called
liturgically conditioned preaching as a locus of divine
encounter.

The word ' liturgy ' is particularly understood to mean the
prescribed words and actions of the Church in the Holy
Communion. The adjective ' liturgical ' however is now
broadly employed as describing any set forms or formulas
appointed for common worship. It is true that, at the other
end of the scale, one of the reforming movements within the
Roman Catholic Church uses the word ' liturgy ' with a
refreshing and Scriptural comprehensiveness to cover the
whole life and work of the Church—its *leitourgia*.

It is in the first two senses that the word is used in these
chapters.

There are churches—there are certainly sects in plenty—
that would rightly disclaim the description of their worship
as liturgical. The Reformed Churches, however, no less than
the Lutheran and Anglican branches of the Church, can and

ought properly to speak of their liturgy. With them the *ipsissima verba* are not appointed; the action is so, whether the pattern is faithfully adhered to or not. And it is the shape of the action that signalizes the character of a liturgy.

Its liturgical forms mark and make a church's style. Indeed they indicate most of the things that can be known about a church. No church, it is true, imagines that God's dealings with men are wholly canalized within the forms of the Church's common prayer. On the other hand no one who stands unmistakably within the New Testament tradition questions that the Church's common prayer is a way of God's appointment, so honoured by the early Church as to be built from the very start into the accepted practice of all Christians. A. G. Hebert is certainly correct when, in raising the question as to how God's truth in Christ is mediated to us:

How far by means of a ritual, and in a liturgy? How far as a revelation of truth addressed to the mind? How far in the religious experience of the soul?

he comments:

It has been common for Christianity to be regarded as a system of belief, or else as a way of holiness for the individual; thus the formal liturgy of the Church comes to be disparaged as an external act, less spiritual than the private prayer in which the individual holds communion with God. But in the patristic period there can be no question that the common prayer of the Church holds the primary place, and provides the setting in which the dogma is seen in its true perspective, and in which the individual drops into his place as a member of the worshipping body.

There is no gainsaying this. The liturgy and that understanding of the Church which is expressed by saying that the Church is Christ's Body, go together. Indeed it is the recovery of emphasis upon the Body—so needful in the over-individualized Christianity of the modern West—which has occasioned the world-wide liturgical movement of this century by inevitable correlation. For these two things go naturally, if not inevitably, together.

What we are concerned with in the present study is the fact that it is in the context of the Church's common worship that preaching normally takes place, and that preaching affects and is affected by its context of praise and prayer.

This relationship of preaching and common prayer is traditional. It is true that at the first beginnings of the Church the propaganda preaching, while it appealed to the Old Testament Scriptures, was not associated with acts of worship. This was to be expected. The Book of Acts presents pictures of the primitive preaching in the open air, as on Mars Hill, when anything beyond a simple testimony was out of the question. Whether within the churches there was at first a rule against praying in the presence of catechumens is evidently debatable.[1]

What is certain, however, is that quite early the liturgy had developed a general pattern and even particular forms wholly familiar to modern worshippers, to part of which catechumens were admitted. It is moving to think that prayers which are part of our Holy Communion service link us directly with the Church of the earliest centuries.

The idea of the Lamb of God seems early to have inspired a special devotion in the Syrian Church. The *Gloria in excelsis* is held to have been used in the Eastern Churches as early as the third century. While it is possible that certain of the adorations in early liturgies derive from the Book of Revelation, the possibility cannot be ruled out that the derivation is in the other direction from a liturgy to the book, and that elements in the vision of the Apocalypse were actually

---

[1] Gregory Dix thinks there was, while Reginald Fuller holds that the instances Dix adduces were really exceptions. *Vide* Dix, *The Shape of the Liturgy*, pp. 17, 447, and Fuller, *What Is Liturgical Preaching?* (London, 1957).

liturgically inspired.[1] The introduction itself, 'I was in the Spirit on the Lord's day', suggests an intense and exalted recollection of familiar offices of common prayer and sacrament.

Within the pattern of worship in the Eastern liturgies, the ceremonial carrying in of the Gospel Book (the so-called 'Little Entrance') betokens the importance attached to the written Word, regarded, as Miss Underhill reminds us, as representing Christ himself.[2] Even in the early days there were, it seems, two aspects of this relationship.

In general the unity of idea in any single service of worship was ensured by the fact that devotions as well as the sermon were theologically controlled. 'O God the Saviour, God of the Universe, Lord and Fashioner of all things, Begetter of the Only-Begotten, Who hast begotten the living and true Expression (of Thyself), Who didst send Him for the rescue of the human race . . .'—such is the manner and content of early liturgical devotions. This may not be the natural language, though it is still ostensibly the thought-form, of the common prayer of the twentieth century, yet beside it much of the public devotion of churches with loose doctrinal standards seems weak-kneed. In them the air of sentimentality and subjectiveness is pervasive, and these defects owe much to the fact that the service is theologically invertebrate or at least diffuse. A certain unity may be, indeed inevitably will be, imposed upon a service by the mood of the minister, but this is a very different quality from the solid objective unity imposed on it by the overriding interest of systematic doctrine. It is this latter which unquestionably marks the early liturgies and which surely ought to mark all Christian *common prayer*. There may well be somewhat qualified norms for private devotion. All this is in general.

[1] Massey H. Shepherd, *The Paschal Liturgy and the Apocalypse* (London, 1960).

[2] *Worship*, ch. vii, p. 131.

In particular, the lections and presumably the exposition, if any, seem to have been controlled by that serial pattern which nowadays we call the Christian Year. It has been suggested[1] that the Gospel according to St. Mark, on the internal evidence of the book itself and on that of the typographical alignment in the oldest manuscripts, was compiled as a series of lections corresponding to the general framework of the Jewish cycle, and, so to speak, baptizing that usage into Christ—a purpose, if this were indeed one of its purposes, in no way incompatible with this Gospel's other supposed employment as a catechetical manual. It has also been argued that St. John's Gospel is an extended Christian commentary on the triennial synagogue lectionary, with especial reference to the cycle of festivals.[2]

Whatever be the final verdict on such theories, there is no question that, as there early grew up a framework for the service, there also grew up a framework for the year. Preaching, so far as its theme is determined by this framework, may be termed liturgically controlled preaching.

## II. THE WORD IN SCRIPTURE AS INTEGRAL

In the understanding of the Reformed Churches the relationship of Word and sacraments is intimate. The Word of God is integral in the service. It is not merely that there can be no sacrament without the operation of the divine Word, that Word which created the heavens and the earth and 'came as flesh' in first-century Palestine; it is not only that, as Queen Elizabeth I put it (following Calvin, following Augustine):

[1] *Vide* Archbishop Philip Carrington, *The Primitive Christian Calendar* (Cambridge, 1952).

[2] Aileen Guilding, *The Fourth Gospel and Jewish Worship* (Oxford, 1960).

'Twas God the Word that spake it,
He took the bread and brake it;
And what the Word did make it,
That I believe, and take it.[1]

It is more. It is that the Word spoken in lections and sermon
or in other ways corresponding to a sermon is necessary for
that *explicit faith* which the Reformers rightly stressed and
which, in the twentieth century, certain reforming movements even in the Roman Catholic Church have been seeking to recover for that Communion.[2]

The relationship of sermon to common prayer has not
always been rightly understood. Instead of a duet there has
been a kind of duel. Among churchmen there are always
some in whom the prophetic genius, and others in whom
the cultic gift is the more highly developed. It is true that
the degree of tension in older Israel between prophet and
priest was at one time grossly exaggerated. The Book of
Psalms, locked as it was into the heart of the cult itself,
clearly reflects both the prophetic and the priestly witness.

Nevertheless the tension is not entirely fanciful; and it
persists throughout religious history. Parallels occur in the
Jewish Church. In the Jewish services in Germany during
the Middle Ages, it seems, unofficial poetic interpolations
into the liturgical structure so reduced the time left for
preaching that no record appears of notable Jewish preachers
there, while in Spain Jewish preaching flourished in the
setting of a simpler rite. A similar situation arose in the
Christian Eastern Church. In Byzantium cultic magnificence
coincided with a general famine of the preached word.[3]

If these are symptoms of an inherent tendency to tension

[1] Quoted in T. S. Garrett's *The Liturgy of the Church of South
India* (Madras and London, 2nd ed. 1954), p. 31.

[2] Cf. E. B. Koenker, *The Liturgical Renaissance in the Roman
Catholic Church* (U.S.A, 1954).

[3] Dix, op. cit, p. 473.

or relative exclusion, the tendency is there in history because it is present in the human heart. The cultic mind stresses the importance of the right formula, the prophetic one the importance of the right will. The one will incline to exalt the appropriate action regarded as effectual *ex opere operato*, the other will require, in response to proffered pardon, the inner contrition known to God alone. The peril that lies concealed for the ritualist is that the will may be exercised in the performance of the ritual movement without being brought to bear in the realm of real encounter which is expressed and sacramentally realized in the ritual movement. The kind of preacher who magnifies the prophetic office but has a weak sense of cult will sometimes be found to have a well-developed doctrine of individual salvation together with a deficient doctrine of the Church and the Kingdom.

The occasion of these differing emphases is commonly, and quite practically, located in the individual's temperament, tradition, or skill. If a man is in the fluent sense a 'born preacher' he will incline to magnify the preaching office, to the relative detriment of the age-long forms of common prayer, or else to regard the devotional service as a means of conditioning the hearer to receive the sermon. If he is not by nature a preacher, he may be found to undervalue the pulpit and to ask with Professor Stalker in a bygone generation: 'We know how many sermons are preached every Sunday; does anyone know how many are listened to?' and thereafter to seek out for himself a liturgical hiding-place; the Tractarian Movement was a veritable godsend to many a clergyman who had nothing to say or, if he had, did not know how to say it.

The fruitful preacher, however, is seldom the one who is born fluent. He is of those who come to be preachers as the fruit of the Holy Spirit's travail, accepting the acknowledged hard work, study, trial, error, adventure, as well as that temptation to personal discouragement which must always be concealed from a congregation but is none the less always involved in the article of being set apart as a preacher.[1]

No doubt cultic religion does present itself as more comfortable than a prophetic faith which is so largely compact of conscience and existential tension. It is nevertheless profoundly unwise to underrate the significance of classical rituals and forms of faith and worship. The classical liturgies, being theologically full-orbed, automatically make good the lacunae that will be found in a preacher's mind and choice of theme, or indeed in the thought of a whole generation. Therefore in times of limited vision (as the medieval age was in one way and the humanist in another) a richly doctrinal liturgy will preserve in relatively clear focus some picture of the full and saving faith. In Old Testament Israel, it was by reason of its very conservativeness that the cult was in this way to prove a blessing to Israel. It ensured an unbroken witness.[2]

However, when the heavens did break and God's rain fell, the vital spiritual movements in Israel took place outside the orbit of cultic activities.

Wisely, in our system today, these movements belong integrally together, the movements of the Spirit in preaching and in common prayer. It is preaching which gives contemporary significance to the ancient words of liturgical prayer, so that, when the Church at Holy Communion prays: 'Lamb of God that takest away the sins of the world, have mercy upon us', it is a real and not a merely liturgical world that is livingly present to our praying minds.

The Word of the Bible does more than this. Within the

[1] Appreciation of sermons is not always articulate. As to this, the late Professor James Stalker once wrote that people 'pay no compliments to their daily bread'.

[2] *Vide* T. C. Vriezen, *Outline of Old Testament Theology* (Oxford, 1958), p. 29.

service it exercises a guardian's office. A padre during the First World War, when asked what he preached about, replied: 'Oh, I give Church teaching.' 'Church teaching' in the sense in which he employed the term was something for which quite certainly no honest exegetical warrant could be discovered in the Bible. At this point there has already opened that rift which ultimately divides churches, those on the one hand (numerically strong and influential though they be) which make a gospel of non-Scriptural sacraments, and those on the other which humbly accept the sacraments of the Gospel. In the former the word of the Bible has not been given 'free course' as, among other things, the guardian and test of the transmitted truth.

It is true that the Church is the interpreter of the Bible. But the Bible is also the interpreter of the Church. When this its true function is denied it, the liturgy itself becomes schismatically dismembered or deformed. The development of the cult of the Blessed Virgin and the theological enormities of the medieval centuries were followed necessarily by a progressive dislocation of liturgy and lectionary.[1]

Thus the liturgy is not safe without the Word, nor the Word without the liturgy, more especially during the generations or ages when there is no 'open vision'. The Word—whether read, preached, or prayed—is the Word of encounter. It is a means of a holy and august friendship. And this implies, for the Body (the Church), whatever it signifies for the individual, something we can only conveniently call liturgy—a form of common eucharistic or eucharistically patterned prayer. If it be true on the earthly level that 'friendship should be surrounded with ceremonies and respects', how incomparably more should it be so in this friendship, this encounter of God with his Church. There fore, though all our responses are but 'shy gestures' which

[1] *Vide* Allan McArthur, *The Christian Year and Lectionary Reform* (London, 1958).

must fail to express not only the worship that is due but even that which is felt, yet we can do no other than kneel and bow and use the holiest words we know. This is how the liturgies were born, and when, in our Reformed freedom of use, we prepare our services today after the received pattern, this is how they must be born again. These too are the fruit of the Word of encounter.

The service, then, is one and indivisible, with the Word of God both read and preached integral in its articulation. One part of it, badly handled, will adversely condition the response to other parts. Nevertheless each part, confession of sin, preaching, adoration, or any other, is there in its own right and for no ulterior end. Prayer, for example, or the singing of a hymn, are never to be regarded as a means of preparing people so that the sermon shall make its maximum impact. To treat the forms of the worship of God as psychological techniques is to introduce into the service an element of falsity already so considerable that, if it is not recognized for what it is, it will quickly become total.

### III. THE WORD IN SCRIPTURE AS PIVOTAL

It has become part of the Reformed tradition that the Church, in providing services for every kind of office and occasion, should offer these as normative and not, as to detail, obligatory. It is obvious that, in the context of this liturgical freedom, the relationship of the sermon and the prayers does not look after itself. It requires to be managed. It was the distinguished architect, Frank Lloyd Wright, who wrote: 'The first condition of homeliness, as it seems to me, is that any building that is built should love the ground on which it stands.'

That is a wise thing beautifully expressed. And the same could be said of the sermon: it should love the ground on which it stands, the soil of Scripture, the Scripturally conditioned worship. It should grow out of what has gone before and lead on to what comes after.

It is a pity, or so at least it seems to some, that in so many churches the Reformed order of morning service (which, even when Holy Communion is not celebrated, is a stripped form of the ancient eucharistic pattern) is dislocated by abstracting the sermon from its proper and natural place closely following the reading of the Scriptures, and transferring it to the end of the service. Lections and sermon, taken together, are pivotal in the articulation of the threefold shape of the service.

It is true that the parts of the liturgy are variously described as having a twofold form, the *synaxis* followed by the *eucharist,* that is to say, the ' liturgy of the catechumens ' (or ' liturgy of the Word ') followed by the ' liturgy of the faithful '. It is entirely a question of different titles.

Certainly in the formative days of the service nothing seems normally to have preceded the lections.[1] God had to speak before man could respond. Later innovations were to alter the accepted norm, differently in different branches of the Church. In the Celtic Churches the purgative act of confession of sin was held to be an essential preliminary to the hearing of the Word of God and the appropriate acts of worship that followed it.[2] To describe the service, therefore, in terms of a twofold division leaves obscured one essential aspect of the relatively simple logic of modern public worship; and it will probably be found that average worshippers more readily grasp the significance of the service of common prayer when they see it as a threefold action.

In the first essential act, our humble approach to Almighty God (not indeed of our own choosing but of his prevenient leading), we acknowledge what God is and what we are. It

[1] *Vide* Dix, op. cit., p. 455 and note.
[2] *Vide* Duncan Macgregor, *Early Scottish Worship* (Edinburgh, 1896).

is true that, coming, as we do, tarnished by the dust and soil of the world and certainly with impaired spiritual vision, this is not an acknowledgement we can begin adequately to make at all except so far as the Holy Spirit enables us to make it. It ought also to be remembered by those who prepare the Church's prayers that the primary recognition is not the recognition of ourselves as sinners but as *creatures*. 'We are the people of his pasture, and the sheep of his hand.' Without this primary *theological* recognition (which is the essential want of our age and the preacher's first preoccupation, since there is no reform that does not depend ultimately on this first reform) there is no meaning whatsoever in the confession of sin. Apart from God there is no such thing as morality though there are still policies of social convenience.

In the second essential act of the service the Word of God is heard in Scripture and sermon, by which we mean the vertical inbreak of the Word of God who is eternal, therefore forever contemporary, and who speaks to 'each in his own tongue' as at the first Pentecost.

These two acts together, shot through with intercession, comprise the liturgy of the catechumens.

The third act, to which all else leads, is the liturgy 'of the Upper Room' or 'of the faithful'—the Communion, whether in the eucharistic actions or, if there be no sacramental elements, in that diverse traffic of devotion that follows as response to the Word of God—the belief, adoration, thankful remembrance, oblation, intercession, and remembrance of the communion of saints.

Such is broadly the pattern of action in every great liturgy of the Christian Churches, Eastern, Roman, Gallican, Celtic, and Reformed. By this continuing pattern, and even in many details, as when we say the 'Lord have mercy' the 'Lift up your hearts', the threefold 'Holy', the 'Lamb of God' and the 'Blessed is He . . .' with 'Hosanna', we are at one with the ages very near to the beginnings of the faith.

D

Central and pivotal in that traffic of exposure and response is the Word of God in lections and sermon.

## IV. A THEOLOGICAL FRAMEWORK

If, then, the eucharistic structure of public worship be observed and if that structure be aligned from Sunday to Sunday to conform with the Christian Year, certain conclusions will follow.

For one thing, the preacher will find himself preaching within a definitely *theological* framework and thus meeting the essential needs of the age he lives in. These needs are not met either by 'tranquillizer religion' or by morality. It always has been the preacher's duty to work within the framework of the massive and objective truth of the Gospel. Morality can never stand on its own feet. The preacher's task, said John Oman, is 'not merely to commend what is pious but to manifest what is true'.[1] That judgement was soundly Christian. The Christian Gospel is not a set of ideals but a proclamation of facts. Indeed one of the sorriest bunglings in our Christian analysis of the situation in any age would be to fail to understand that the fundamental locus of concern is never primarily a moral landslide, real and disturbing as that can be, but a collapse of *ultimate*—that is to say *theological*—understanding. We are not present in church as idealists wishing that something might be, but as believers acknowledging that something *is*. In a sermon the element of proclamation is always a stronger thing than exhortation, as theology is stronger than pietism. It is this ringing note of facts that is characteristic of the liturgies in their fontal and uncorrupted forms, and by comparison we can now see that it is in this respect as in others that certain churches have been passing through a period of relative disablement from which however there are signs that they may yet emerge.

[1] *Concerning the Ministry* (London, 1936), p. 239.

Moral teaching is of course necessary, but it must arise out of theological understanding and find its sanction in the fact of a God whose nature, as the Bible unceasingly insists, is to be a Will.

It has been asserted[1] that the catastrophic collapse of morals in the time of Edward VI in England was due to the sudden cessation, because of the Reformation, of the ethical preaching of the friars and others. Such assertions require to be accepted with some caution. That was an age of the loosening of a long-standing social fabric, and correspondingly of the sanctions associated with it, and that fabric was to a great extent theologically based. It was not merely that Edward was a minor and 'Woe to the land that's governed by a child!' It was, in a metaphorical and therefore profounder sense, that 'authority forgets a dying king', in other words the Church, the former source of authority, had too long been in a dying condition. It was the temporary weakening of the *theological* authority that weakened, as always it must, the *moral* understanding.

There is a place, and it is a large place, for ethical teaching, but that teaching must arise out of theological understanding and find its sanction in the fact of a God whose nature, as the Bible unremittingly insists, is to be a Will. Indeed the test of all ethical homilies is a rigorous one, and it is this: if a Stoic teacher could have taught substantially what the sermon teaches, if in fact he could have spoken your sermon, even— as at many points he could—to the extent of quoting Jesus as a moral teacher, then, in that form, that particular sermon has no place in the Christian pulpit. That pulpit was consecrated to other uses, and everything there spoken is spoken, not merely in the quite explicit context of the theological Gospel, but in such a way that people understand and feel that, subtly yet radically, that Gospel has introduced a new ethic: always it is 'a new commandment I give unto you '.

[1] *Vide* Dix, op. cit., pp. 596-7.

In the New Testament the Spirit of Christ is not something to be cultivated but someone to be received. Outside the Kingdom, loving one's neighbour means that *natural* pity or compassion are allowed to express themselves, or, if they are momentarily defective, that one should still do from duty what one cannot do from the heart. It is still one's own heart that is expected to feel and one's own will that wills. Inside the Kingdom, loving one's neighbour is something that Christ does in and through the servant. It is the beautiful mystery of an inner direction and an inner obedience. This is why there must always be a difference, indefinable but subtly felt, between good works that spring from a sense of duty (which at its highest may have a Stoic nobility and at its lowest may be an inverted expression of the infantile prohibitive conscience), and those that are Christ's own action in someone through whom he has elected to work.

An illustration of this is to be found in Laurens van der Post's book *The Dark Eye in Africa*. In it he describes how, at the moment of the liquidation of the Dutch sovereignty in Indonesia, the puzzled Governor-General pointed out to him all that had been done for the colonial people—by hospitals, communications, all the resources of a technical civilization, and asked: ' Can you tell me why they want us to go? ', and the answer was: ' I'm afraid it is because you've never had the right look in the eye when you spoke to them.'[1] Great issues can turn on a thing as simple and as profound as that. The dutiful watchfulness of the conscientious administrator is in a different spiritual category from that other spirit which cannot be imitated but only received by humble obedience— that Spirit which is not our own natural compassion heightened to a degree but that supernatural thing, Christ's own compassion working through his ' Body ', the Church.

In this field of factual proclamation it is significant to compare what has happened in the realm of ultimate beliefs in

[1] Quoted by Theodore Wesel, in *Ecumenical Review*, April 1957.

Western Christendom and in Soviet Russia. 'Hegel', writes Bertrand Russell, 'thought of nations as the vehicles of dialectic movement; Marx substituted classes. He disclaimed always all ethical or humanitarian reasons for preferring socialism or taking the side of the wage-earner; he maintained, not that this side was ethically better, but that it was the side taken by the dialectic in its wholly deterministic movement.'[1]

Here is a secularized, inexact, but very striking form of a doctrine of election which has occasioned the same kind of extraordinary release of energy as sprang from the Calvinistic exposition of the Biblical doctrine of election several centuries earlier. An individualistic religious predestination had given place to a secularized social determinism. From this viewpoint Marxist philosophy looks very like Calvinism without God.

What, for the present discussion, is the force of this? It means that the real strength of Communism lies in the committed minorities who accept *an assertion concerning the nature of things*. They do not say: 'We must bring about the collapse of capitalist societies.' They say: 'In the nature of things *laissez faire* societies are doomed to collapse.'[2]

It would be precarious to press this parallel too far. Of one thing however there can be little doubt. There is in the human soul at all times a demand for what some would call metaphysical assurance or, at a deeper level, the wish to know to whom the title-deeds of the universe belong. It is to some extent strange, because, contrary to what is sometimes affirmed, this metaphysical uneasiness is only temporarily mitigated by social prosperity, in fact until the first enchantment has worn off.

[1] *History of Western Philosophy* (London, 1946), pp. 815-6.
[2] Referring to the immense Russian confidence in the scientific field, an article in the *Scotsman*, 21 February 1958, comments: 'This is not a post-Sputnik mentality. It is the mentality that produced the Sputnik.'

The many and genuine boons of a welfare state create the atmosphere at first of a honeymoon. The human race however has a long memory, longer than that of the individual. Perhaps this is why prosperity always makes people more than a little uneasy. They court it and do not entirely trust it. Their instinct is a true one. Every minister with any wide experience of people in the varied situations of our everchanging fortunes learns that people are much more at ease and much more themselves when they are coping with some element of hazard. The essential need is not for fortune but for something to live for and a faith to teach one what that something is. To this we must return, in a different context, later.

The disclosure of faith's facts, then, is basic. As early as the time of the First World War P. T. Forsyth was warning the churches: 'theology is greater than philanthropy, because men do not know where they are. They are only steering by dead reckoning—when anything may happen. But theology is "taking the sun".'[1]

Theological facts are the Bible's all-encompassing theme. It is therefore what we are *required* to preach. The rediscovery of this has involved the Biblical expositor in our day with what is virtually, for him, a new task, since the humanist surrogate for revealed religion—ethical idealism—has long and deeply conditioned the thinking of religious people. It has so dominated pulpits in Europe and America that many people read into the Bible, and many preachers preach out of the Bible, little else but a humane idealism.

One may take as a laboratory test the Parable of the Prodigal Son—what Dr. W. R. Maltby used to say ought to be called the parable of the prodigal father. How does the average reader interpret such a story? Does he not almost

[1] An American description of an atheist is that he is one who is 'all dressed up and nowhere to go'. John Buchan described him as a person with no invisible means of support.

inevitably think of it as a tale of moral reform? Accidental details appear to support this reading: for instance, the prodigal ' wasted his substance in riotous living . . .' Is not ' this thy son which hath devoured thy substance with harlots? ' But this is not radical interpretation. The far country, as Jesus knew, need not be very far off geographically, and it is possibly not to any great extent populated by harlots.

The Gospel of God's grace in judgement and mercy takes deeper soundings than this. The prodigal ' came to himself '. Nowhere did Jesus say he came to himself when he decided to ' turn over a new leaf ' morally and become a good boy according to the code. His conversion was not *primarily* a matter of moral reform at all, whatever it may have been secondarily. It is written very clearly in the parable: he ' came to himself ' when he decided: ' I will arise and go to my father . . .'

The significance of such a statement, in the evangelist's intention, is theological. It also indicates the Bible's view of sin. Sin is fundamentally a religious before ever it is a moral revolt. It is the repudiation of divine authority, the stubborn resolution to be self-determining, in fact to be one's own god. ' Father! ' (the last time he will ever, as he imagines, require to use that bitterly constraining word) ' I am of age. Give me my portion. From today I manage my own affairs . . .' It was this that Jesus indicated to be sin, before ever any formal breaking of the code had taken place. Sin was not the breaking of the law, it was the making of one's own law. Sin, that is to say, was not primarily immorality, it was irreligion. It was not first of all dirt, but a well-scrubbed and highly-polished pride. Therefore repentance was not first of all moral reform but religious obedience. It lay in saying: ' I will arise and go to my father . . .'

These are the Bible's comments on our superficial diagnoses; and they represent an incomparably profounder reading of the human situation. It means that the current

crisis is not moral first of all but cultural and more particularly religious. It is the slow corrosion of man's primal
awareness of the Ultimate Will beyond our creaturely will.

In general it should be obvious on the face of it that the
preacher's office is to preach theologically, even when he is
dealing with the most pedestrian of moral virtues, if any such
there be. If the so-called 'Christian ethic' is in fact nothing
more and nothing less than the precipitate in conduct of the
individual's personal relationship with God in Christ, then
the moral issue is a highly dramatic and a deeply personal
one. Indeed it becomes possible to say that apart from the
fact of God nothing is either good or evil morally, but that
good and evil become terms referring merely to convenience
and comfort, much as one might speak of a good chair, or a
good, or bad, motor-car.

## V. THE COMPLETE BIBLICAL SCOPE

Clearly something more requires to be said and the Christian Year reminds us what that something is. It is this: that
Christian truth is not this or that Christian truth but the Faith
in its totality and sweep. It begins with St. John's prologue
reinterpreting the doctrine of creation which had proclaimed
that this world is not self-explanatory—the attestation of its
origins is not stamped upon the face of Nature itself (thus
putting so-called natural theology in its place). It moves
through all the mighty acts of the old dispensation and the
new, expressed in type and anti-type, to that consummation
expressed in the doctrine of the Second Coming, insisting as
it in its turn does that the destination, and therefore the road
on which to walk, are not proclaimed upon the face of
Nature itself.

It is theoretically obvious that preaching should cover this
ground. Most of us come to learn, however—and some learn
it slowly and some late—that truth is a corporate possession,

and each individual left to himself enjoys only a fragment of it. In practice, therefore, without the discipline of a system, the ground will not be covered by one in fifty or a hundred preachers.

To one preacher the Resurrection means everything, to another the Cross. One has had experiences that lead him to speak much of special providences, to another the Incarnation is the sovereign revelation. One conducts a healing and helping ministry, another specializes in the life of devotion.

Such accidental emphases can be a strength and a weakness. They can be a strength since a man is not likely to interest others in something he is not interested in himself, still less in something that is utterly unreal to him. Clearly there is a young man's Christ and an old man's Christ, and also the young man's Christ is different from the young woman's. Henry Drummond was right in warning that if you find a young man professing the religion of his maiden aunt, then he is guilty of cant. Genuine flame has a way of kindling others and nothing else will.

Nevertheless such idiosyncracies of interest may disable a whole ministry in the long run. Unless something is done to correct the tendency, the special interest will act as a magnetic centre in the mind, attracting into its field, for study, only one class of matter, therefore failing to extend the area of interest and knowledge. A well-known modern preacher once confessed that in a severe illness he discovered that the faith he had preached was inadequate to support himself. And it came to him that he had too little rested on the New Testament promise of the Holy Spirit.

It is this peculiarly personal nature of a man's faith that accounts for the fact that as you read the Bible—or indeed any serious literature—while chapter after chapter may interest you, it does not provoke you to stop reading and think. But turn a page and in a moment you are reaching for your pencil and note book. You have lighted on something that is germane to your preoccupying intellectual or spiritual interest.

This defect, which lies not in the fact of the limited experience but in the inability to progress beyond it, may be rooted in a lack of humility, in that pure egocentricity which cannot trace the seal of validity in anything beyond one's own limited vision; or it may be a defect due to an ill-cultivated imagination—hence the great value for preachers of being continually soaked in the genuine and abiding classics of literature. To no preacher ought it to be possible to say, as the Abbé Arnaud said to Diderot: 'You possess the reverse of dramatic talent; the dramatist must transform himself into all characters; you, on the contrary, transform them into yourself.'[1]

It ought not to be possible because above all the Bible is exactly the kind of literature that kindles and enriches the imagination. The movement of Biblical scholarship in our time is opportune and enriching. Like all good things, it carries with it also a peril—the peril that the minister may too much read about the Bible and about the Biblical doctrines and be himself too little soaked in the Bible itself. When the devout reader in an earlier generation read about Judas Iscariot, he knew himself to be Judas Iscariot, or if he read about Peter, he *was* Peter. This is the kind of imagination that interprets experience, and helps a man to discover that he has actually had a wider experience than he had fully realized. It is such imagination that makes for great preaching. Alexander Whyte's sermons are illustrations of this.

Throughout a ministry these magnetic centres of the mind ought to go on multiplying through experience and imagination. Such centres are themselves the source of magnetic attraction to the hearer. Where they are too few in number and too limited in scope the ministry requires to be part of a geographical circuit. It cannot be long sustained in one place.

[1] C. A. Sainte-Beuve, *Portraits of Men* (Essay on Diderot).

VI. THE SCOPE OF THE LITURGY

One has only to make a quick mental survey of the classical structures of Christian worship to see how this corporate possession of truth which has passed into liturgy and lectionary makes good the deficiencies of the individual's vision. 'The liturgy', says Guardini (and the remark applies to any adequate act of corporate weekly worship), 'condenses into prayer the entire body of religious truth. Indeed it is nothing else but truth expressed in terms of prayer.'[1]

The eucharistic prayer is clearly Trinitarian in emphasis and form. The *Sanctus* (the threefold HOLY, with its reminiscence of Isaiah vi), the *Anamnesis* (the memorial of Christ), and the *Epiclesis* (the invoking of the Father to send the Holy Spirit) form a Trinitarian pattern not as a matter of mere artistry, for which there is no place in prayer, but because Christian prayer must strike these notes by reason of its own inherent nature.[2]

The service as a whole is comprised of a Trinitarian framework, richly clothed with detail. In one form or another it commences with Genesis (in the recognition of the Creator), passes through Old Covenant to New Covenant, moves on to the work of the Holy Spirit in intercession and holy task, and closes (since the whole service takes place, as does the Christian life, in the condition of eschatological tension between the first and second advents) on the final note of the Book of Revelation—'Even so, come, Lord Jesus.'

If this is true of any one service, how much more is this entire body of truth filled out, developed, and substantiated in the course of the Church's Year. Indeed it is matter of tested experience that through the faithful use of the full theological frame of worship a man comes gradually to enter into

[1] Romano Guardini, *The Spirit of Worship* (London ed., 1937), p. 15.
[2] *Vide* the Communion Office in *The Book of Common Order* (1940), and especially (for the eschatological conclusion) the Order for use at the General Assembly of the Church of Scotland.

that part of the Christian experience which at first was beyond the scope of his tradition and vision.

If Christmas is the festival of the Incarnation, the splendour of such an occasion is little satisfied by a sermon which attempts to conjure up the spirit of brotherhood by idealistic appeal. Here again there is a right and a wrong way of stating a truth. Sentiment is an essential part of God's providence for men. But when sentiment is made a substitute for theological understanding, it is subtly perverted into that sentimentality which was for a time a characteristic vice of churches.

Because of this it was long forgotten that in the New Testament neither God's fatherhood nor man's brotherhood are generalized conceptions, as if the latter were assumed to be of the natural order of things.

God is first of all 'the Father of our Lord Jesus Christ'. This is how his fatherhood first comes fully into view, and it is when we are 'in Christ' that he becomes, for all practical purposes, '*our* Father which art in heaven'. In the same way, Jesus is our 'elder brother', and in a quite new and different way it is 'in Christ' that we become aware of being 'brothers one of another'.

It is not the echo of a fine desire but the ring of a still finer reality that is sounded in the ancient prayers which celebrate the august event of Incarnation:

While all things abode in tranquil silence and that night was in the midst of her swift course, Thine Almighty Word, O Lord, leapt down out of Thy royal throne, Alleluia![1]

The theme of the Christmas preaching is an act of God. People spend much time asking the wrong questions. The classic question of doubting humanity has always been: 'What is God like?' But this question cannot be answered in a void. The Gospels make a different approach. They

[1] *Sarum Breviary*. Antiphon to the *Benedictus* for the Octave of the Nativity.

begin with the succinct. They dare to face the scandal of the particular (why after all should it be assumed that God can best be expressed in the abstract when he himself has always chosen to express himself in the concrete?). They ask therefore about the 'Holy Thing' that came to Galilee: 'Whose son is he?'

The Nativity story, whatever else it is, is the theological answer to that question in a significant picture. St. Luke shows it in his own way. St. Matthew shows it in his, by portraying the three gifts brought by the Magi—the gold as the gift of tribute for a monarch, the frankincense as indicating one to whom divine worship is due, and the myrrh in adumbration of the Passion. It is theological throughout.

The question 'Whose son is he?' is raised again in the story of Jesus in the Temple at the age of twelve or thirteen, and he himself is shown as answering it: 'Wist ye not that I must be about *my Father's* business?' It is raised again in the narratives of the Jordan baptism, and answered: 'This is my beloved Son . . .' It is raised more than once in the narrative of the ministry of Jesus, and always in a context which indicates that the question is significant and not genealogical. And at the end the Gentile world is portrayed giving its first tentative answer (the new children of the Kingdom who were shortly to be coming from the north and south and east and west to eat bread in the Kingdom) when the centurion at the cross is made to say: 'Truly this man was the Son of God.'

These, in the Gospels, are not casual references. They are theological and are intended by the evangelists to carry the full weight of theological significance. A Christmas without this emphasis may be celebrated within the Church, but it is not the Christmas of the Church. Not only so. It is possible to *follow* the yearly scheme of lections and themes, even selecting texts in themselves suitable for the day, without however preaching in terms of the essential Gospel.

Take, by the way of illustration, the text 'sown in weakness . . . raised in power' (1 Cor. xv. 43). Here is an antithesis vivid and suggestive which sets the mind pondering. If a preacher feels drawn to preach on that, how is he to do it? The easy way—neatly cutting the text out of its context with the scalpel of desperation on a Saturday night—is to treat the passage as if it were a description of a natural phenomenon, a principle inherent in Nature, and to proceed by itemizing the ways in which this phenomenon may be observed, winding up of course with the Cross and Resurrection. For instance, you may illustrate the suggestion in the text from the life of a child 'sown in weakness . . . raised in power', developing from primal helplessness to the fulness of rich and virile manhood; or you may instance interesting enterprises which from inconspicuous beginnings have become world forces, 'sown in weakness . . . raised in power', the Christian Church being far and away the most striking of these. Thus, when you conclude with the Cross and Resurrection, the impression is apt to be created that this last is only another illustration of a truth that is somehow in the nature of things. But this, surely, is not the Gospel, and may come very near to being the opposite of the Gospel.

There is another way of expounding the text. It is infinitely more difficult, yet, for the building of faith and of the knowledge of God, infinitely more rewarding. It is to preach the Incarnation, Cross, and Resurrection throughout the sermon, and *within that universe of discourse* to discuss the other instances, now quite clearly with a deepened if not indeed with a quite different reference. The sowing in utter weakness of a child and the raising in the power of manhood, is that nothing more after all than a remarkable natural phenomenon? Growth from what, to what, for what? What is man? During the war a shell-shocked soldier had lost his memory. He was no longer aware even of his own identity. At an army boxing tournament at which a great concourse of men from different units were present, he was led in to the boxing ring in the hope that someone who had served with him would recognize him and offer him the first essential clue to mental health, knowledge of identity. But no one knew him. After a while, frustrated and desperate, the man threw out his hands in a passion of appeal: 'Will no one tell me who I am?' It is an ultimate question. What is man? Natural science speaks of natural origins. The faith of the Kingdom, the font, the sacrament of the broken bread and the one cup, all speak of a very different understanding of this human being as 'sown in weakness . . . raised in power'. It is, even in the world of succession, a super-natural sowing and raising; and it is this that we preach.

The distinction here being drawn is not fanciful. It is that which distinguishes the Bible from other literatures. Our time has seen much use of a cliché, sentimental to a degree, which assumes that God loves all men because 'there is good in all'. The Parable of the Lost Sheep is thus sometimes preached under the title of 'The worth of human personality'. But this, if it were true, would not be *grace*. The attitude represents the vestigial survival of a now threadbare humanism which was bound to wear thin because it had no solid doctrinal basis.

It is not (I think it is Professor H. H. Farmer who has well made the point) that God loves people because they have some supposed worth in themselves, but that they have worth entirely because God loves them. This is the reversal of the current assumption. An advertisement appeared in a news paper some years ago, asking for the return of a lost teddy bear. The toy belonged to a little girl and the reward offered was a large one, somewhere in the region of ten pounds It seemed a large reward in the circumstances. But in which of the circumstances? In the circumstances of the market or in the circumstances of the little girl's affections? Certainly it would have been possible even in those days to have bought

as good a teddy for a sum less than that offered for the return
of the old one. What then was the value of the bear? Probably
the longer the little girl had possessed it and the more dis-
reputable in appearance it had become, the less would its
value be in the market and the greater in the eyes of its young
mistress. Clearly the real value of the toy was the value con-
ferred on it by love. And it is not different, it seems, with the
love of God.

'God so loved the world . . .' By this love the world is
both valued and judged. This is not the substitution of one
sentimentalism for another. It does not indicate the kind of
tolerance that might be expected from what someone has
wittily described as 'a Grandfather in heaven'. A grandfather can afford to be tolerant. A father cannot. If God
therefore condoned men's sins, he would not be more loving
but less so. In fact, as has been often said, he would cease to
be God.


VII. LITURGICALLY CONDITIONED PREACHING
    CUMULATIVE

There are patterns and patterns. It is possible to create the
impression of systematic preaching by announcing in one's
Parish Magazine a forthcoming series of sermons on incidents
in the Gospels under the titles of:

> 'The woman with the water-pot'
> 'The man with the pitcher'
> 'The boy with the picnic basket'
> 'The girl with the beauty compact'

and even within that framework to preach quite earnestly
and systematically on great Gospel themes such as judgement, grace, and justification. Nevertheless (and it is a point
we must return to in a later chapter) this type of approach
is inclined to lead to sermons that might be described as
humanism in a cassock.

In the same way the parables of Jesus will constantly provoke the preacher to see in them meanings and suggestions beyond the evangelists' first intention.[1] And why not? As Professor C. H. Dodd has said: ' By all means draw from the parables any ' lesson ' they may suggest, provided it is not incongruous with what we may learn of their original intention. We shall not easily exhaust their meaning. But the Gospels do not offer us in the first place tales to point a moral. They interpret life to us, by initiating us into a situation in which, as Christians believe, the eternal was uniquely manifested in time . . .'[2]

It should seem obvious that in order to understand the parables, it is necessary to place oneself, so to speak, in a first-century pew and imagine oneself hearing them for the first time in that setting and those circumstances. It is fairly certain that to those who first heard them the parables were not only parables of Jesus, they were also parables about Christ. The real peril today, when the preacher substitutes a superficial system of attractive titles for the essential system of the Gospel year, is that many listeners are so poor in Christian truth that they will not know that they have been the victims, at worst, of a preacher's vanity (for this is the swiftest road to preaching popularity of a sort), and, at best, of his lack of purpose.

Whatever be the preaching this age welcomes, the preaching it needs must be systematic. Both the method and the effect will be long-term. This is the nature of liturgically controlled preaching. ' No thought can think ', wrote W. P. Ker, ' if it is perpetually broken up into small fragments, little glittering fanciful images.'[3] The system of Christian thought provides no exception to this rule. It has, even in our time, suffered grievously from fragmentation. It requires

[1] *Vide* ch. III.
[2] *The Parables of the Kingdom* (London, 1935), p. vi.
[3] *Vide* Cecil Day Lewis, *The Poetic Image* (London, 1947), p. 53.

E

now to be seen again in its historic sweep and its spiritual scope.[1]

The effect of such preaching is not merely cumulative during the course of the sermon itself but over the course of the weeks and months.

The novice has begun to be a preacher when he has proved himself able to preach effectively through a Gospel from Christmas to Easter, using as the hard bony structure of the course the climacterics in our Lord's life and ministry, noting the Old Testament types and their significance as a means of interpreting the New Israel or Covenant People in Christ, and sensing throughout the divine action in the varied events: the purposeful humility of the Incarnation; the 'silent years' of preparation in Nazareth about which the Gospels tell us nothing except by inference; the visit to the Temple at the age of twelve; the waiting and preparation while the gusty winds of the Baptist's preaching are searching out the dusty corners of rabbinism, of uncriticized code and ritual religion; the empty stage when the Baptist was taken and Jesus heard the insistent call-bell; the baptism at Jordan in which we see Christ as Mediator, in our own baptism and in much else; the testing of vocation in the wilderness with its type-significance; all the challenge to the Church today in the calling of the Twelve—significant number of the

[1] *Vide Book of Discipline*, 1560, XI: 'Farther, we think it a thing most expedient and necessary that every Church have a Bible in English, and that the people be commanded to convene to hear the plain reading or interpretation of the Scriptures, as the Church shall appoint; so that, by frequent reading, this gross ignorance, which in the cursed papistry hath overflown all, may partly be removed. We think it most expedient that the Scriptures be read in order, that is, that some one book of the Old and the New Testament be begun and orderly read to the end. And the same we judge of preaching, where the minister for the most part remaineth in one place. For this skipping and divagation from place to place of the Scripture, be it in reading or be it in preaching, we judge not so profitable to edify the Church, as the continual following of a text.'

Tribes—their training in prayer and their field-training during the Galilean mission; the climacteric at Caesarea with all that is implied by being a confessional Church; the so-called Transfiguration (how vividly modern that narrative is, with its suggestion of how men always seek the way out by any means short of the one that is radical, hoping to make the world 'safe for democracy by the middle way of the law' and, when that proves only partially effective, by the leadership of their passing prophets, while the perennial need is for a Saviour and a radical and inward conversion); then to the solemn Passion events which we are never to deal with sentimentally, as if it were our office as a Church to pity Christ, while the Gospels portray his Passion as the expression of his divine pity for us and of *his* all-conquering purpose—'Sing my tongue how glorious battle glorious victory became', and so to Easter and (both in the Gospel narratives and today) to the Real Presence in the Blessed Sacrament, to Ascension, and to Pentecost—'the earnest of an inheritance'.

To see all this and to see it in terms of today is to be a preacher. But this is epic work. This kind of preparation is not done in carpet slippers, nor does a congregation hear it as the old lady liked to hear sermons when she said of her minister that she liked his preaching because, if your mind wandered, it was quite easy to pick up the thread when you began to pay attention again.

In all this the parochial preacher has a supreme advantage over the peripatetic evangelist. Where the Christian Year is observed—which is the same as saying where the Biblical revelation is set forth in its full range and its consecutive order—instead of the fragmented glittering images that Ker referred to there comes into being a close-knit framework of truth. What Mozart said in the field of music of even an extended symphony, 'the best of all is to hear it all at once', becomes true also of the Gospel. It is when the hearer has been exposed Sunday by Sunday to the living Word of God until at last the whole revelation is his in its serial completeness, that, on any one Sunday, however limited the particular theme of that day, the overtones are all the time heard. These overtones—the various messages of all the other Sundays—are also being made explicit in the prayers.

During the year it is all presented serially. On any one Sunday, and indeed at any one moment of vital hearing, 'one hears it all at once'.

# CHAPTER THREE

# THE IMAGE

. . . how last unfold
The secrets of another world, perhaps
Not lawful to reveal? Yet for thy good
This is dispensed, and what surmounts the reach
Of human sense, I shall delineate so,
By lik'ning spiritual to corporal forms ,
As may express them best: though what if earth
Be but the shadow of heav'n, and things therein
Each to other like, more than on earth is thought?
MILTON, *Paradise Lost*, Bk. V, 569.

## I. THE PROBLEM OF LANGUAGE

We turn now to consider the language of encounter. In one form or another this will be the theme of the present and the following chapter.

'God will do nothing', says Amos, 'but he revealeth his secrets unto his servants the prophets' (iii. 7). The question is: What currency of discourse is this language of revelation and communication? It is clear that there is a problem here and that it has two aspects.

One aspect of the problem becomes apparent in the very article of preaching itself. It is the familiar problem of communication: 'Preach in language that we can understand!' No one imagines that this problem is new in the twentieth century. It is age-long and epidemic, if not indeed endemic.

It is too simple an answer to say that the break in communication *must* be the preacher's fault. Sometimes it is so. A person who shoots above the target, James Denney used to warn, merely proves that he cannot shoot. The great preachers have always had the common touch. When Jesus spoke of his 'yoke', he was making contact by means of a metaphor already familiar to his hearers. Everyone knew the phrase 'the yoke of the Law'. St. Paul, in using technical terms of Jewish religion, phrases from hymns, and possibly from liturgies of mystery religions, was only being to the Greeks a Greek, to the Jews a Jew, in order to 'save some'. St. Columba in his missionary preaching introduced Christ by saying: 'Christ is *my* druid.' It was his point of contact. And every successful preacher in history has spoken first so as to be understood.[1]

Nevertheless there can be a deafness that is the hearer's disability if not actually the hearer's fault: 'having ears they hear not', or else they have, as the Bible puts it, 'itching ears'. Itching ears are selective; they do not hear the thing that is important but only the thing that is sensational or superficially amusing. There are other disabilities which appear, in this age of history, to be almost constitutional.

If the preacher's problem were merely how to preach so as to be understood, it would be a simple one. The difficulty is more subtle. It is how to discover a language which, being understood, is also capable of supporting the gravamen, the seriousness, and the mystery of the Gospel. The question is whether any language can be commensurate with either the weight of this Gospel of God's grace or the sheer facts of the human predicament, unless it is saturated with the sense of mystery as well as of history. That must be discourse of such a kind that, when men hear it, they are aware of the Unseen or, even more explicitly, they encounter God. If the language of the street is fitted to do this, then let the language of the street be the tongue of the pulpit. If not, then we must examine this task of communication. On the preacher's side the problem is how to speak in words which will be under-

[1] In reply to a question of mine, a successful Scottish preacher, Dr. R. T. Cameron, said he had tried to keep three aims before him in preaching, namely, to be heard, to be understood, and to be helpful.

stood, and in the same moment be the occasion of encounter in the terms—and these the full terms—of the Gospel.

Behind this question however lies another. Before there was communication from the pulpit throughout the centuries there was revelation to someone prior—some apostle, thinker, saint, man of prayer. Once again : ' God does nothing but he first reveals it to his servants the prophets.' This primary vision is of course renewed still whenever and wherever someone is aware of being directly dealt with by God through the Holy Spirit, whether through the sermon or not. What is the language of that primary encounter? How is God known, or rather more truly how, after one has become conscious of being known *by* God (for that is what religious experience means), does one express this experience so as to transmit its significance? What is the language of primary encounter?

There can be little doubt of the answer. It is the image.


## II. THE IMAGE AS THE LANGUAGE OF ENCOUNTER

' What ', thought Alice as she looked over her sister's shoulder just before her Adventures began, ' what is the use of a book without pictures or conversations? ' For its relevance to the problem of communication the question is well worth pondering. The Bible, the book of the divine encounter, is *par excellence* the book of pictures and conversations. It describes God's age-long dialogue with men and provokes them to participate in that dialogue still.

On the one hand this encounter is understood by men as involving a word of command to do something and to be something, and from this standpoint God is known through his self-manifestation as Holy and Sovereign Will. God's ' mighty acts ' both demand and make possible a response. On that side the precipitate of encounter is an action.

But suppose you try to describe the God you are aware of,

how are you to do it? Why, you make an image. The Old
Testament law forbade the making of a graven image, but
it did not and properly could not forbid picture-thinking—
the making of a mental image, since there was no other way
that men could with any sense of reality think about God.
This is as true of civilized as of primitive men.

Wherever one may turn, one will never get past this
necessity, that the language of the Unseen is an image, and
that preaching to be effective involves learning its effective
use. 'Wisdom', said Yeats, 'speaks first in images.' 'I hear
voices', said Shaw's St. Joan, 'telling me what to do. They
come from God.' Robert retorted: 'They come from your
imagination.' 'Of course,' Joan replied. 'That is how the
messages of God come to us.' Poulangey interjects:
'Checkmate!'

Exactly. It is checkmate. Abstract language is, it is true,
the means by which the report of the supposed encounter
with God is criticized with a view to checking its accuracy.
It is not the natural language of the encounter itself. The
mental precipitate of God's dealings with men is always an
image.

The New Testament and the Old alike, as we all well
know, are full of this. The type, the parable, the metaphor,
pictures of the Good Shepherd, the Sovereign God, the
descending dove, the cloud, the tongues of fire, the smoke
in the Temple, the Light, the Living Water, and that
strange wayfaring Figure, no longer shaped or coloured or
clad according to the previously known categories of recognition, of whom the Gospels record that he appeared to the
disciples 'in another form' and 'they knew not that it was
Jesus'—all this and much more like it is, as we all know,
wholly characteristic of the Bible's way of speaking of the
'mystery', the opened secret of the Gospel. Not surprisingly
it is also the characteristic language of the liturgies.

The language of faith, then, is the image. This fact is of

first-class importance for the preacher, both as to his interpretations of the Bible and his preaching technique. When he speaks of God and tries to describe God's ways of dealing with men, he speaks in images, analogies, parables, metaphors, paradigms, both Biblical and extra-Biblical. Metaphor is in fact *the sacrament of the imagination*.

This is the language of which the great preachers have always been masters. Yet this apparent necessity of religious images has been subjected to rigorous criticism and analysis.

'What was puzzling us', wrote Dr. Austin Farrer in his Bampton Lectures, 'was the function of images in revealed truth. The scandal appeared to be, that we cannot point away from the revealed images to an imageless or " straight " truth which the images signify.' 'We cannot bypass the images to seize an imageless truth.'[1] And again, putting it another way: 'It is only in being aware of something finite as an analogy of God that we begin to be aware of God at all.'[2]

It must be noted also that under certain conditions the image has power to move men beyond any other currency of concepts; in the field of faith the most obvious example of this is the fact that the cross itself, from being an historical object, becomes in the preacher's hands a theological image.

'If I were asked', wrote Professor Macneile Dixon, 'what has been the most powerful force in the making of history, you would probably judge me of unbalanced mind were I to answer, as I should have to answer, metaphor, figurative expression. It is by imagination that men have lived; imagination rules all our lives. The human mind is not, as philosophers would have you think, a debating hall, but a picture gallery. Around it hang our similes, our concepts. The tyranny of the concept, as, for example, the concept of the universe as a machine . . . this tyranny of the concept is one

[1] *The Glass of Vision* (London, 1948), Lecture iv.
[2] Ibid., Lecture vi.

from which the human mind never escapes . . . Metaphor is the essence of religion and poetry . . . Nor does science escape from this entanglement . . .'[1]

Even the world of history finds itself involved in the world of metaphor. In passage after passage of the Bible it is actual historical events, or sometimes (as in the Epistle to the Hebrews) liturgical uses, that are employed as images of heavenly things or types of some past or future 'mighty act' of God. To take only one illustration, the historical crossing of Jordan into the Promised Land of Canaan became an image that has played a long and very potent role in theology and in popular devotion. All this is of course commonplace to students of the Bible. There can be no understanding of this Book except by recognizing that its language is, as indeed we should have expected, a language of the imagination—that of images—even when it is a quite concrete past instance of God's dealings which has become to the eye of faith a prefiguration of a later encounter. This remains the language by which the preacher still describes God's encounter with men, and there is no other.

III. THE IMAGE AS A LANGUAGE OF ACCOMMODATION

What then is the difficulty of preaching? Is it that the stage-conventions of faith, so to speak, remain the same for preachers but ordinary folk no longer accept or understand them?

There is truth in this, but far less than has sometimes been asserted. It is true that in the field of thought generally the once accepted apparatus of imaginative expression has to some extent disintegrated. The classical images which comprised an accepted convention in poetry and prose alike right down to the nineteenth century, the mythological figurations familiar to readers of Milton, Keats, and Shelley, flash with

[1] *The Human Situation* (London, 1937), ch. iii.

but pale portent across the minds of casual readers today; they are not understood. The Biblical images have suffered also, though in a different way.

This, if it were the only difficulty, would be remediable by teaching. The *malaise* is more fundamental. The situation is paralleled by Shakespeare's plays; although the vast majority of Shakespeare's readers have known nothing about that audience and theatre for which he wrote, yet they have enjoyed his plays. 'And', A. C. Bradley says, 'if they have enjoyed without fully understanding, it was for want of imagination and of knowledge of human nature, and not from ignorance of the conditions under which his plays were produced.'[1]

Much the same can be said about the reading of the Bible and Bible-centred preaching. Given imagination, the Bible will still be found to 'ring the bell'. Yes, given imagination! Hence the insistence of religious analysts today that there can be no enduring revival of faith without the recovery of a feeling for poetry. The imagination is the realm where speechless man meets unspeakable God and visualizes the encounter in images. The image is only a language of accommodation, as all language must be that attempts to speak of the ineffable, and there is no satisfactory alternative to it. The failure fully to realize this and to come to terms with it is one of the reasons why sermons sometimes fail.

Yet this was once a natural tongue on the part both of preacher and hearer. The old lady who said of a preacher's over-lengthy introduction, that he had taken so long to lay the cloth that she had quite lost appetite for the meal, would have no great difficulty in reading the Bible. She spoke its language.

Is there not a further occasion of difficulty in the way both of preacher and hearer, the responsibility for removing which

[1] A. C. Bradley, *Oxford Lectures on Poetry* (London, 1914), Lecture on 'Shakespeare's Theatre Audience'.

lies squarely with the Church's scholars? Disagreement
persists among scholars as to which parts of the Bible are
imaginative—theology in pictures, including historical
events that are used as pictures pointing beyond the actual
event itself—and which parts are more or less uncomplicated
narrative, in no sense heightened, in no sense figurative or
pre-figurative. As students of the Bible well know, the past
forty years have witnessed an epoch-making movement of
Biblical scholarship which has constantly seemed to promise
a generally accepted apparatus for interpreting the Scriptures,
making it possible for the reader to see the unity of the Bible,
the coherence and congruity of its imaginative structure.
That promise lies still in the future. The scholars are not as
yet agreed.

It is not difficult to see why. On the one hand modern New
Testament scholarship has reacted rightly against Origenistic
forms of allegorizing the Scriptures (though Origen did
clearly distinguish between the plain historical sense and the
typological sense which he read into the text as a means of
arriving at the spiritual sense which would be the basis of
the preacher's application). An apparent example of allegorizing is to say that in the Parable of the Prodigal Son, the
father *stands for* God, the prodigal son for fallen man; at
that point it becomes difficult to see what the servants
in the house stand for. A parable is not an allegory
in this strict sense at all; yet at the same time no one can
read of the father in the parable without thinking of God
in terms of the father's love and actions. This reaction therefore is understandable but must not be allowed to become
perverse.

Equally understandable is the reaction against extremes of
typological method which interpret the Gospels as if every
passage and almost every verse had, in the evangelist's intention, a *typical* significance. The moderate typologist finds in
the Gospels the story of our Lord's life told in terms of the

story of the Old Israel or people of God of the Old Testament; or alternatively he sees in the Gospel story our Lord choosing to live his life in terms of the experience of the Old Israel, choosing twelve disciples, for instance, in conscious anti-type to the original twelve tribes—all this with a view to drawing out a Christological significance, namely, that in Jesus Christ there has come into being the New Israel of the New Covenant.[1]

As to some typological interpretations there is room for difference of opinion. The real confusion arises at the point where the two methods are mistakenly identified and the typologist is accused, sometimes quite wrongfully, of allegorizing.

## IV. THE PLACE OF IMAGINATION IN PREACHING

What then is the preacher to do so long as the debate of the scholars is inconclusive? The answer surely is plain. He must enter into the Bible's imagination and he must use his own.

This question can be posed in another way. First of all, if there was undeniably an intimate connexion between the thought-forms of the New and Old Testaments (just as there was an intimate link between the realities these forms attempted to express), what did the New Testament forms mean in the intention of the evangelist? Very close to this question is another: What did the very first readers, preachers, or hearers understand the evangelist to be saying? Allowing for a degree of blurring, incidental to all verbal transmission, the answer to the two questions can be assumed to be fairly similar.

The Bible describes the series of historical events and liturgical forms which, however concrete and actual they are in the Old Testament, become a constellation of images

[1] A thoroughgoing and, in places, strained application of the typo-logical method is to be found in the works of Dr. Austin Farrer.

when they are used in the New Testament to express the nature of the New Covenant.

To say this does not solve the preacher's problem, but it does in part define it. It enables him, in some degree, to enter into the mind of a first-century convert whose ways of religious thinking are being moulded by the Gospel but whose forms of thought are derived from the Old Testament.[1] What is any given passage from a Gospel likely to have meant to such a hearer? It cannot be too strongly said that to arrive at an answer scholarship is essential. Equally, to arrive at an answer scholarship is not enough. To the Bible's imagination must be added the preacher's.

E. V. Rieu, in the introduction to his translation of *The Four Gospels*, writes of the danger that ' as a preliminary to the study of the Gospels, too large a dose of Form-Criticism might well reduce one to the condition of a man who stands before Raphael and keeps on asking where the artist got his paints. I myself ', he goes on, ' avoided this unprofitable state of mind by translating the Gospels first and as far as possible shutting my eyes to all that had been written on the subject. At a later stage I availed myself of the labours of professional workers in the field in order to correct my mistakes and to check the validity of my first impressions against the findings of modern scholarship.'[2]

This is a method well worth while for the preacher, to go first to the text and to draw certain conclusions which can afterwards be checked by all the available evidences of scholarship. Interestingly the grand and awe-inspiring line of the story stands out with historical clarity and convincingness. It presents itself as having a firm bony structure in a series of impressive climacterics, such as the Baptism in Jordan and the Transfiguration on the Mount. At the same time there is always an impression, more or less explicit, of a

[1] See also ch. II, section VII.
[2] Op. cit., p. xix.

Christological pattern. Put differently, the sensitive reader, inevitably conscious of the solid historical framework, is none the less haunted by the sense that the historic facts are made, so to speak, to wear a halo, as the figures in a Renaissance painting do, and this in the interest of the Christological proclamation.

The two white figures at the tomb on the morning of the Resurrection are clearly not in the region of simple biography but of dogmatic significance. These figures signify something and are intended by the evangelist to convey some part of the truth concerning Jesus Christ. What they signify is the task of the scholars to tell us. Some have thought that they are related in this world of images to the other sets of two figures, earlier at the Mount of Transfiguration (the Law and the Prophets, the characteristic representatives of the Old Covenant witnessing to Christ) and later at the vision of the Ascension, so that in the mouth of at least two witnesses 'it shall be established'. Certainly no two witnesses could be more significant in the eyes of Jews and proselytes than these; nor would it be out of character to represent these witnesses at the place of the Ascension vision since Christ's Ascension and exaltation loomed so largely, along with the Resurrection, in the thought and in the liturgies of the early Church. One thing stands out, that at such a place as this in the narrative we are in the realm of Christology as well as, in some sort, of biography.

Or what is purported by the different, and in quite salient points contradictory, narratives of the Resurrection in the Gospels? Surely that the real yet wholly indefinable fact of the Resurrection is in each instance set forth to draw out some special significance which it held for the evangelist, and that each did this in his own way. If this is so, the fact of the disparities in the narrative no longer constitutes a problem of history and a stumbling-block to faith, as if we are necessarily led to impugn the accuracy of all evangelists because we can be sure of none; what we now have is an enrichment, in that we are given, as it were, several different expositions, each treating the same mighty theme in its own characteristic way, and each supplementing the others.

What then we appear to have in the Gospels, both at the one moment, in the selfsame chapter and verse, is something which after all is wholly characteristic of the Christian way of looking at things: we have at the same moment portraits of Jesus and images of Christ. I shall come to illustrations of this shortly, in a slightly different context.

But if, first, the preacher's task is to understand what the evangelist intended to say—what God was saying through the evangelist to that early generation of Christians—thus entering into the Biblical imagination, the preacher's task is, secondly, to try to understand what God is saying through a particular passage of Scripture to this generation of ours; in other words, the preacher's imagination is the place where the eternal Word in the earlier historic Word becomes the contemporary Word.

There can be no denying this. The poverty of the preacher's imagination spells the death of preaching, and it is the best of the scholars who are quickest to recognize this. 'We need more grammarian's funerals!' one of them said. W. M. Macgregor quotes Professor A. B. Bruce's distinction between verbal and real exegesis, and goes on to say that a student who is a mere exegete in the formal sense may still be, ' so far as the Divine meaning is concerned, entirely an outsider; whereas, with vastly less of preparatory work, a man of living mind might have got to grips with what is central. That is apparent in many of the mighties; Luther was technically a very defective scholar according to modern standards, but he had a certain congruity of nature and experience with Paul which made vital understanding possible.'[1]

Professor Vriezen also finely says:

[1] *For Christ and the Kingdom* (London, 1932), ch. III.

The fact that he, the preacher, has been touched by the spiritual content of the Bible makes him completely dependent on the Biblical message; but this obedience to the subject-matter in some respects frees him from the letter, from the form in which the message comes to him. He may grasp the message at various points, wherever he discovers it (cf. e.g. the sermon on faith in Heb. xi, but especially the way in which Jesus Christ freely uses Scriptural texts); by understanding the matter one may rise above the Word as a historical datum; and exactly in that way one may fulfil the Word . . .'[1]

There is an interesting parallel in the preaching of the Celtic Church, in which the eucharistic sermon—usually an exposition of the Gospel for the day—normally had a three-fold structure (after the introduction): the literal meaning (*sensus historicus*), the spiritual or mystical meaning (*sensus spiritalis*), and the ethical meaning (*sensus ethicus moralis*). 'The excellence of a sermon . . . was popularly gauged (and the ancient Scots were great critics of sermons) by the depth and originality of the *sense* that the preacher drew from the passage under the second head.'[2]

It is not only the preacher who will thus use his imagination. Inevitably the kindled hearer will do the same, as indeed he must have done from the beginning.

What did the first-century hearer make of the story of Martha and Mary (Luke x. 38 ff.)? Most certainly not what the uninstructed modern reader does. Today one man will interpret it differently from another and a woman will interpret it differently from a man. A man, being inherently more philosophical than a woman, will see in it a picture of the supposed, certainly widely accepted, antithesis between 'the material' and 'the spiritual'; the Bible however is not concerned primarily with the debate between Zeno and

---

[1] *An Outline of Old Testament Theology* (Oxford, 1958), ch. IV.

[2] Duncan Macgregor, *Early Scottish Worship*, Lee Lecture, 1895 (Edinburgh).

Epicurus, at least in the terms in which they respectively posited the issue; and one can rest assured that the evangelists did not waste their time teaching a lesson, or representing Jesus as teaching a lesson, that a high-minded Stoic might have taught. A woman, on the other hand, being practical and domestic, will—for a near certainty—see herself in the role of Martha the hostess and will be more than inclined to sympathize with her until she remembers, a little uneasily, that it was after all Jesus who gently rebuked Martha and commended Mary.

Whatever the evangelist's first intention may have been in disclosing this tiny incident in his Gospel, it is not difficult to put oneself into the position of a Gentile woman convert in some congregation built on the solid foundation of St. Paul's missionary preaching. Such a woman had no ' works ' to bring before God as plea for acceptance, as the Jew had for many centuries. She had not borne the ' burden and heat of the day ' like the workers in the parable who objected to the late-comers (as the Gentiles were late-comers) receiving on equal terms the inheritance of God's promises. She had accepted a Gospel which taught that a man—or a woman— was ' justified ' before God (by God's own gracious decision) by ' faith alone ' in response to ' grace alone '. When this parable was first read to her, it is not impossible that she saw and interpreted it in terms of her situation and of the teaching of the Gospel as she had received it, and said to herself gratefully: ' Martha? that is what the Jew is like in his faith —like the older sister " cumbered about much serving "; but Mary, sitting at Jesus' feet and simply trusting in his word— that is me, the Gentile, the younger, new come to the Kingdom.'

This form of image, of the older and the younger, of obedience as the old Israel understood it and as the new Israel knew it, runs through the parables of Jesus, as its theme runs through the mighty preaching of St. Paul, of Luther, of

Calvin, and of the Church, wherever the Church has been true to the Biblical Gospel.

Or, for fuller measure, picture, later still, how preacher or hearer might find the other story of Martha and Mary—that in the Gospel according to St. John—to be kindling to faith and thought. When Jesus had come to the home at Bethany, Martha 'went her way, and called Mary her sister secretly, saying, The Master is come, and calleth for thee '.[1] Is that a story or an image? It is a story and something more than a story. In the hands of the preacher it becomes an image. The Advent was, in one form or another, the great theme of the Church, as still it is. The basic message of the Old Testament could be expressed in four words: 'The Master is coming!' Through great tracts of the Old Testament writings there is that note of hope and expectancy, the sound of distant and approaching feet. 'There shall come forth a root out of the stem of Jesse.'[2] 'The Lord . . . shall suddenly come to his temple . . . and who may abide the day of his coming? '[3] Always that is the burden of the Old Testament announcement: 'The Master is coming!' But the New Testament announcement, the good news which the apostolic preaching heralded as with the sound of trumpets, had the grander note of completion: 'The Master is come and summoneth thee!'

Was it possible for the idea of 'coming' and even the idea of summoning to have other than theological significance for the earliest Christians? The moment the word was spoken, it must have become, on the preacher's lips, in the hearer's imagination, or both, an *image* of truth.

The preacher of course has a duty to be clear, and to make it clear to his hearers, when he is genuinely interpreting the evangelist's thought with scholarly integrity and when (and

[1] John xi. 28.
[2] Isa. xi. 1.
[3] Mal. iii. 1, 2.

this is also legitimate) he is using a passage (a fragment of a story, for instance) to illustrate a truth by analogy.

One can only surmise what the earliest hearers of that most Jewish of Gospels, the Gospel according to St. John, made of the profoundly imaginative narrative of the Resurrection —the precipitate once more of an experience of encounter indescribable by ordinary narrative modes, and, within that grand picture, what they made of the vivid glimpse of John and Peter racing to the tomb and finding it empty. The evangelist appears to be concerned with evidences in the manner peculiar to this Gospel, but he also appears here, as throughout his Gospel, to be closely interested in the relationship of these two apostles within the Christian community and to that community.[1] If so, here is a question of distribution of functions, and a possible lesson on the Body and the members.

But it is part of the power and endless resource of the Scriptures that they are constantly throwing up meanings beyond the prime meaning of the sacred writer. There may well have flashed through the mind of some listening Jew the picture of an earlier and different race to a place of ashes, of that ritual race in fact which took place as part of the Temple cult, in which the priests on duty raced to the altar and mounted the ramp, and the one who reached 'within four cubits (off the altar)' had the honour of emptying the ashes of the previous day's sacrifice.[2] And, in that age of sacrifice, was there not a vivid antithesis in the two pictures, the daily race connected with the Temple sacrifices which required to be ever renewed because the atonement had to be made again and again, and now the race to the place of Christ's sacrifice in which there were no ashes because now the final sacrifice had been made 'once and for all'? It is not

[1] *Vide* Oscar Cullman, *Peter: Disciple, Apostle, Martyr* (Eng. ed. London, 1953), pp. 28 ff.

[2] *Vide* Raphael Patai, *Man and Temple* (London, 1947), ch. III, p. 73.

suggested that such meanings were within the evangelist's intention at this point but only that this might so easily have occurred to the listener then, just as it is the kind of way in which the mind of the preacher handling the Scriptures works, by analogy, antithesis, image. Certainly it is of clear intention and on the grand scale that the author of the Epistle to the Hebrews employs precisely these liturgical usages of the Old Covenant as images to express the truth of the New.

Leaving aside all images *beyond* the Biblical writers' intentions such as occur to any preacher who illustrates the Bible from the Bible by using, for instance, narratives metaphorically, the authenticated images are ubiquitous. Some of them are now 'dead images'—that is to say, they have become dead *as images* because their social reference is no longer familiar. In its earlier use in the field of religion the word *redemption* instantly conjured up a vision of the slave-market. The word has to some extent lost force because it no longer does so. The word, as an *image*, is maimed.

## V. THE MAIMING AND RECOVERY OF THE IMAGE

The problem seems to be that whereas in the first centuries the images, because they were familiar currency, expressed and interpreted the mystery, today we have to interpret the images. We appear to be in the position of Abraham Lincoln who as a young attorney would say of a case he was pleading: 'If I can divest this case of technicalities, I think I can swing it to the jury.' The difference between Lincoln and the Christian preacher is simply this, that we cannot wholly dispense with the technicalities.

The New Testament is written in a highly technical language of Christological images. Nowhere do we escape this difficulty. We could avoid it if the Gospel dealt in any other matter than theology. In theology, almost alone, it cannot be avoided. The parable of the Labourers in the Vine-yard[1] may indeed be used to instigate a discussion on social justice, but only properly on that theme if its primary theological significance has first been read. But what is that significance?

Is it that our Lord was illustrating the grand theme of God's grace and favour, by the analogy of the parable point-ing to the late-comers, the Gentiles, who none the less are to share the promises of the New Covenant on equal terms with the faithful of the older Israel who had borne the full burden and heat of the day (the yoke of the Law) under the older dispensation? Certainly no discussion on the vital question of social justice is ever likely to be worth while which does not look at the issue from this viewpoint: How does God deal with men, and how does he measure, by a strict foot-rule or by the eye of grace? Through the theology the ethic also comes to life in the image.

This kind of language, then, is indissociable from any discussion of matters of faith. It is a language that can be explained. It cannot be dispensed with. Our preaching ministry depends on making it live.

Let us then ask once more, and this in the interest of the proclamation: what is the function of the image, what is its effect, and what does it achieve? Why is it the natural language of preaching, this magic of metaphor, simile, parable, or paradigm—this image?

The function and the effect are very much what Coleridge described them to be where, in his *Poetical Tenets*, he tells us of the compact which he and Wordsworth made with each other, whereby they were each to contribute to a joint volume of poems (the abortive *Lyrical Ballads*): 'it was agreed', wrote Coleridge, ' that my endeavours should be directed to persons and characters supernatural, or at least romantic; yet so as to transfer from our inward nature a human interest

[1] Matt. xx.

and a semblance of truth sufficient to procure for these shadows of the imagination that willing suspension of disbelief for the moment which constitutes poetic faith.'[1]

Notice the general idea: Coleridge's images were designed to make *shadowy* things *real*.

Mr. Wordsworth, on the other hand, was to propose to himself as his object, to give the charm of novelty to things of every day, and to excite a feeling analogous to the supernatural, by awakening the mind's attention from the natural lethargy of custom, and directing it to the loveliness and the wonders of the world before us, an inexhaustible treasure, but for which, in consequence of the film of familiarity and selfish solicitude, we have eyes, yet see not, ears that hear not, and hearts that neither feel nor understand.

Wordsworth's images were thus designed to disclose the *supernatural* in the *visible*.

The compact between these two choice and so differently gifted minds is suggestive of what does in fact happen when the relationship between the seen and the Unseen finds expression in the consecrated images of faith. The effect is to make the supernatural homely and the homely supernatural.

Either way there will be a sense of revelation. Everyday things, trees and factories, duty and duty-rosters, even trouble, temptation, pain, and, of course, other people (however difficult!) will, to the hearer's surprise, take on a novel and supernatural significance; the world itself will be seen not only as this ' vale of soul-making ', but as a house of many splendours. On the other hand things people had counted as supernatural, austere, distant, or possibly merely awesome, will become personal, accessible, and intimately real. Indeed the higher and truer the presentation of the Gospel and the more candidly it is accepted, the more the experience should feel like a home-coming after long wandering. This always

[1] Coleridge, *Poetical Tenets*.

is in fact the experience of the convert, as it is of the Christian penitent in all his comings back to God from week to week and day to day. As the medieval phrase has it, in the Blessed Sacrament 'the Lord Jesus is full homely to us'.

Once more, how is this to be done in view of the benumbing of the feeling for poetry and the decline in vitality in some of the Biblical images themselves?

There can be little doubt about the answer. The Biblical images themselves can be directly refreshed by personal Christian experience. 'The reason', wrote P. T. Forsyth,[1] 'why so many sermons are found uninteresting is not always due to the dullness of the preacher . . . It is because it, the miracle of grace, seems foreign to us. It is like reading a guide-book if you have never been in the country. I take down my Baedeker in the winter and read it with the greatest delight, because I know the country. If I had not been there I should find it the dreariest reading. Why do not people read the Bible more? Because they have not been in that country. There is no experience for it to stir and develop . . .'

It is also true nevertheless that the Biblical message and experience constantly sparks off fresh imaginative forms in the mind of the preacher or hearer, and that the Bible's images are refreshed by being reinterpreted by modern images drawn from contemporary life and experience.

I have watched the faces of the members of a Youth Fellowship in a city parish as a distinguished visiting speaker tried to explain the 'tongues of fire' that 'sat on the heads' of the converts at the first Pentecost. The faces were mostly blank. The young people were trying to grasp it, but the image of the tongues of fire failed to kindle their imaginations. How can we make the spark leap the gap between the Bible account and the modern mind?

In such an instance the one image requires to be interpreted by another. For example: in modern Peru parts of the New

[1] *The Work of Christ* (3rd ed. London, 1946), ch. 1, p. 29.

Testament have been translated into the language of a
Peruvian Indian jungle tribe deep in the ' green hell ' of that
hinterland. A young missionary girl translator was reading
some verses of the translation to a little native group. The
Chief approached and stood listening. Again and again he
asked to have the sentences repeated. At last he exclaimed:
' My heart understands with a leap! ' St. Luke wrote of
' tongues of fire '. The Indian Chief said: ' My heart understands with a leap! '[1] Cultivated cosmopolitan Jerusalem in
the first half of the first century and the Peruvian jungle in
the second half of the twentieth, but the same Word! The
same Holy Spirit witnessing in the heart, the same tingle of
response, but a different image. The history of the Church
is full of such little Pentecosts, and where the story as originally told fails to ring the bell of reality, the image kindled by
the contemporary experience makes the classical image come
alive.

Or take, as an illustration of this necessary technique in
Christian doctrinal preaching, that numinous sixth chapter
of Isaiah, a fruitful matrix (even to the coal upon the
prophet's lips) of many inspired liturgical forms: ' I saw
also the Lord sitting upon a throne, high and lifted up, and
his train filled the temple. Above it stood the seraphims . . .
And one cried unto another, and said, Holy, holy, holy, is the
Lord of hosts: the whole earth is full of his glory . . .' It is
among other things a study in directions. The range of the
prophet's circumspection is impressive. First, like so many,
he looks *around* (Isa. v. 30): ' And if one look unto the land,
behold darkness and sorrow.' From this despairing view he
looks *up*, and sees God high and lifted up, yet very much
Sovereign in the midst of men—' His train filled the temple.'
Thereupon the prophet, like all who have once seen God,
looks *within*, aware at once of his own uncleanness and of

[1] *Vide* article by Clarence Hall on the work of the Summer Institute
of Linguistics, in *Readers' Digest*, April, 1959, p. 159.

God's will to cleanse him. And from that he looks *forward* and sees a task—' Here am I, send me! '

Without that setting in life, the vision is too rarefied, partaking too much of the idea of the ' wholly other ', even (in its imagery of the Temple) too ecclesiastical to make a universal appeal today. The Biblical image is infinitely suggestive, austerely beautiful; but for many hearers it may require to be interpreted by another image more familiar and closer to the primal springs of human feeling. Given this, Isaiah's vision may begin to live for them, and indeed they may discover with surprise that they themselves have actually had constant experience of the Unseen, the nature of which they had not recognized, partly *because the experience was so familiar*, also because, lacking a living language of native imagination, they had no name to give it.

Yet there are, certainly not ordinary, but everyday kinds of experience which may help to interpret and clarify the Biblical one. On the Western seaboard of Scotland, where the sea stretches long arms inland, the sound of the sea is incessant, and if one is not aware of it, it is because it is always there, a kind of atmosphere. One hears the lowing of the cattle, the cry of a mother calling her child, the ring of a spade striking rock. But only in moments of exquisite awareness does one consciously hear the unceasing sea and the winds. It is the very keynote of all sounds, the unremitting background music of everyday life, and for that very reason not consciously noticed. It may be somewhat like that with the sense of God. People notice the immediately engrossing things, the neighbour's chatter, the factory wheels, the radio, but not the ' Holy, holy, holy ', the keynote of the universe. St. John of Patmos would have understood this. He lived as a convict on an island; and the voice of Christ, he said, was ' like the sound of many waters ',— the background music of life in Patmos.

Human nature is so very vulnerable to God. It is in this

conviction born out of experience that we preach. To most people, often quite apart from all churchly stimulus, there come moments of awareness when, looking back, they are conscious that throughout their life there have been over-tones in all their experience—a sense, however ill-defined, of restraints, constraints, and half-glimpsed revelations: they would agree that, in retrospect, there has not been a day in which decisions have been made in which there has not been, however tenuously, a feeling of moral choice. Most people then, do hear, albeit muted and very far away, the 'Holy, holy, holy'. It is this awareness that preaching must make explicit. The everyday image interpreting the sometimes rarefied image of the Bible is one of the means.

In short, whether we preach about unkind gossip or the august mysteries of the Holy Trinity, there should be always a sense of revelation and at the same time a sense of kinship. This point was raised earlier; let us look at it now more closely.

## VI. ELEMENTS OF FAMILIARITY AND SURPRISE

It is possible to preach about the sense of wonder from the numerous texts beginning 'they marvelled'. It is more im-portant to preach so that everyday things come to be viewed with a refreshed sense of wonder. If someone says there is nothing remarkable or supernatural about the impulse to be kind, the answer is that to the Christian it is drenched with the supernatural. When people become aware of so simple a thing as this, it is with a sense of revelation.

This element of surprise in Christian preaching is not after all surprising. People live during so much of their time in a world of illusion that there is an element of surprise when-ever for a moment they see life as it really is. The wish to appear important, the easy drift into the cynical phrase by which morally timid or socially aspiring people try to put themselves on a level with the others by conforming, the living of a great part of life through the illusory medium of a television screen or of the dreams fostered by the popular press, the determination not to be ' had ', not to be a ' sucker ', not to let down one's caste, all this is to live in a world of unreality.

To get at the truth of life, it is frequently necessary to reverse the current clichés and assumptions. For instance, it is constantly assumed and said that empty pews are due to ineffective preaching. But are they? An empty pew may be a symptom of bad sermons on the preacher's part or of a bad conscience on the part of the absentee hearer, who will not risk exposing himself to that Word that is ' quick, and powerful, and sharper than any twoedged sword . . . and is a discerner of the thoughts and intents of the heart '.[1] It is not man's fictions, but truth, which is surprising and challenging. That is why the Gospel came and still comes to men, when it is livingly preached, with a stab and startle of revelation, and at the same time like a coming home.

Consider what the Bible says about rest. Naomi promises Ruth: ' You will find rest in the house of your husband.' Is a minister to tell *that* to the over-driven among the housewives in his congregation? And yet—where are the restless hearts? Where else, as someone once shrewdly commented, is a woman to find rest for a lonely or troubled heart except in the house of her husband? It is true after all! Or think of our Lord's even more strange promise: ' Come, you who are desperately wearied and I will give you rest. Take my yoke on you and my burden . . .' As a recipe for tiredness it sounds fantastic, and yet, as a pragmatic proposition, there is a burden that the selfish always carry, the burden of their never-to-be-appeased desires. On the other hand there are burdens that carry us, and such are the burdens Christ lays upon us, together with his ' yoke ' both to ease the shoulders

[1] Heb. iv. 12.

and to share the carrying. People who are the instruments of Christ's love receive both the strength and the joy. There is no question about this.

> Some folk, you wonder why, love you,
> While you, you wonder why, love none,
> We love, fool, for the good we do,
> Not that which unto us is done.

And to love is to be fulfilled, to have 'rest'. This paradox also is true after all.

Or take the conception of anti-Christ. What does the Bible make of that? If you did not know the Bible (or human nature) you might expect anti-Christ to be something quite obviously devilish, the incarnate opposite of Jesus. Our Lord himself taught very differently, that anti-Christ was something so like Christ that many quite well-intentioned people were in danger of being deceived. 'Many shall come saying, "I am He." *Then* it is time to beware!' Can you apply that? Can you apply it to the Church and to churches? It involves a radical researching of what it means to be Christ and then of what it means to be Christ's and to be Christ's Church. What are the marks, or, as the old phrase had it, the 'notes' of the Church? The protest about continuity and succession will not alone suffice to appease that question. 'Say not to yourselves: "We are children of Abraham."'

Or again, people constantly insist that the Church is pessimistic and unhopeful because of its insistence on man's sinfulness. By contrast, the next moment, you find them protesting, in weak extenuation of some item of conduct, that 'to err is human'. But is it? If Jesus had sinned, H. R. Mackintosh used to insist, he would have been less than human; sin dehumanizes.[1] In fact the image of man as fallen

---

[1] *The Person of Jesus Christ* (Edinburgh, 1912), ch. VI, p. 401.

is the charter of man's dignity. It proclaims the status God willed for man. By asserting that he is fallen, it asserts that his true place is at the higher level.

## VII. MISSIONARY AND APOLOGETIC SIGNIFICANCE

Preaching from within the impressive constellation of Biblical images which characterize the Christian Year, wherever the logical sequence of the earlier lectionaries has not been dislocated, has both a missionary and an apologetic importance. It is here that, so far as the intellectual aspect of communication is concerned, there lies the possibility of making God real to modern people, and this for what at first appears a strange reason, namely, that the poetic or religious image is not misleadingly explicit. It was first of all—under God—a creature of the poet-seer's imagination before ever it became an agent to someone else's and it still leaves something for the Holy Spirit to do through the imagination and experience of the hearer.

The question of the degree of credal explicitness is an important one. Preachers are constantly being warned against preaching abstract sermons, and the instinct behind the warning is a sound one. Abstract description by its very nature destroys the sense of concrete reality. An element abstracted from a total situation and separately described has already subtly altered its character, and when two elements are so abstracted, they take on the character of antinomies. In the actual situation these elements cohere; in the abstraction they appear as contradictions, or at least as uneasy associates. Elements in a true democracy are freedom and authority; in abstraction for purposes of discussion they seem to war with one another, though in a healthy social economy they are held in steady and useful poise—freedom expressing itself in the making and the honouring of good laws. In the same way, in theology, ideas—like the formerly fashionable notions of immanence and transcendence—are difficult to think together in the one moment in their abstract form, yet —if there be truth in the ideas—what they represent must reside harmoniously together in the actual situation embraced by the two words 'God' and 'history'.

One can understand why Joubert advised: 'It is not hard to know God, provided one will not force oneself to define Him.' Now no one supposes that an image attempts to define God. The revealed image hints at reality, with not too broad a hint yet in a way so congruous with experience that it looks and sounds as indeed it is—right. Think of some of the concepts that hang uneasily together in the popular mind— freedom and authority, Providence and life's pain and struggle. Volumes continue to be penned on such themes. How does the Bible deal with them? It speaks in a picture. It says:

For the Lord's portion is his people; Jacob is the lot of his inheritance. He found him in a desert land, and in the waste howling wilderness; he led him about, he instructed him, he kept him as the apple of his eye. As an eagle stirreth up her nest, fluttereth over her young, spreadeth abroad her wings, taketh them, beareth them on her wings: so the Lord alone did lead him, and there was no strange god with him.[1]

Here in the concrete picture the abstract antinomies such as authority and freedom (essential elements in all education), or of Providence on the one hand, and on the other that possibility of error and suffering which is implied in freedom, are resolved in the concrete situation of the Bedouin father leading his boy through the waste and howling wilderness— the only way he will learn: and it is reinforced by the further image of the eagle training her young. The artistic integrity of the whole lies in the fact that it is in the wilderness that

[1] Deut. xxxii, 9-12.

the boy and the father both see illustrated in the eagle and her brood their own situation. And God's dealings with Israel are the type of his dealings with every man.

Here then in this picture is the very challenge and savour of a life that is in any degree to be salty and liveable. Here is the sharp edge of austerity, the stiff resistance of reality. People see the image and instinctively feel: 'That's true to life! That's how life is and that is how it must be, if God's ends are to be secured.'

That there is an apologetic significance in the recovery of Biblical understanding is obvious enough. This imaginative recovery does not by any means remove the 'skandalon' or stumbling-block of the Gospel—the daunting assertion of the Incarnation, for instance. It removes the spurious stumbling-block comprised by misunderstanding of the Bible's forms of thought. The believing, and especially the scholarly, sections of the Church have far outstripped the blind and stumbling religious hesitations of yesterday, though the scars of old controversies survive in vestigial remains. Great numbers of people however have not yet caught up. We once spoke of outworn faith. That is no longer the issue. The problem is to reach the many now well outside the churches who once were clinging to *outworn doubts* and who, finding no solution, have now simply bypassed the issue by giving up thinking of the matter. In preaching nothing will do but a genuinely Biblical—as the literalist was not Biblical—interpretation of the Bible's thought-forms in evangelism, preaching, and Bible study.

T. E. Hulme has pointed out[1] that 'there are certain doctrines which for a particular period seem not doctrines, but inevitable categories of the human mind'. People 'do not see them, but other things through them'. Now it is clear that modern thinking, controlled by these modern categories

[1] In *Speculations*, quoted and discussed by Alan Richardson in his *Christian Apologetics* (London, 1947), ch. III, p. 65.

of the human mind, the moment it is confronted with the exegetical interpretations of fifty or sixty years ago, suffers nothing so much as a wintry sense of unreality, and sometimes very rightly so.

What is the unversed reader to make of the story of the promise of a son (who as we know is to be John Baptist, the 'Great Precursor') to the elderly pair, Zacharias and his wife? Is the untutored reader likely to take the significant point that Zacharias is a priest serving in the courses of the Temple, or to make anything of the assertion that when he is given the promise of a son he is struck dumb?

It is true that there are subsidiary points (important for a particular sermon but subsidiary in the narrative itself) which the preacher can make quite legitimately about the strange story. He can profitably point out that a believing church or a believing man is a witnessing church or man, and that you can test churches by this. A church that is not, to use Chesterton's phrase, 'simply prancing with belief' will be found to be, so far as convincing witness is concerned, dumb. Belief's joy always shows an overplus in some kind of witness.

It is noteworthy that such a manner of interpretation has itself already quitted the dubious ground of pure history and turned the story into one of significance. Was this however the significance which the evangelist himself intended the reader to find in the narrative? It is unlikely.

Certain commentators assert that the evangelist is using an historic form of structure to draw out the *significance* of John Baptist: that the dumbness of the priestly Zacharias stands for the decay of the prophetic spirit in Israel, a prophetic dumbness that was ended only by the emergence of John Baptist, the preparer of the way for the One to come: and that this is typified in the story in the fact that Zacharias regains the power of utterance by speaking the name John.

G

Such interpretation does not of course mean that the narrative is unhistorical; it means that it is dealing with a different history than the modern reader would at first suspect, but one that is essential to the economy of the Gospel —in fact with the two solid historic facts, the decline of prophecy and its rebirth as the prelude to God's mighty acts in Jesus Christ.

Such interpretation may or may not be correct. As to that scholars are not agreed. If it is mistaken, it remains the task of the scholars to tell the preacher what the passage means. Some of the older commentators were content to assert that the aphasia of the old priest was God's judgement on him for his disbelief in the promise of a son. Whatever other interpretation is right, it is certain that this is not. God does not, in that crude way, punish unbelief. God comes down from heaven. And no interpretation can be true to the Bible's own emphasis and method which does not take the story out of the sphere of fairy-story or superstition and into the theological realm which is the realm of faith's creative imagination.

As to this the Western world is still walking the Emmaus Road. Like the disciples to whom Jesus came, people's eyes ' are holden that they cannot see '. This numbing of the sense of the Unseen is one of the road accidents of our time, and it has to do not only with the disturbance of older forms of belief and with the temporary distraction of all the new excitements of material discovery; it has also to do with language and forms of thought.

To become explicit, adoration requires language. Otherwise it remains a vague awareness of the numinous or at best a sense of awe which still requires to be moralized. And the language that alone can express the ' mystery ' or opened secret of the Gospel, rending the Veil of the Unseen, is that which the Bible itself uses, image after consecrated image. The preacher is wise who does not forget that this is also the language of the human heart, of ' the lover and the sage '.

This is why the Eternal Word will be recognized again in the twentieth century in judgement and gracious encounter only where the images of faith are reminted afresh in the glowing crucible of the preacher's mind.

# CHAPTER FOUR

# THE SONG

---

Forget not, brother singer, that though Prose
Can never be too truthful nor too wise
Song is not Truth, nor Wisdom, but the rose
Upon Truth's lips, the light in Wisdom's eyes.

WILLIAM WATSON

## I. LIMITATIONS OF A VERBAL CULTURE

We consider now the Church's song as a vehicle of the Eternal Word.

In primitive religion it was supposedly not the song but song's elder cousin, the dance, that constituted a kind of primitive liturgy—the mimetic dance of the rain-makers or the dance of sheer ecstasy. And then the inevitable accompaniment, the song—the incantation, dirge, charm or paean —sometimes with ecstasy and in course of time with stately and significant ceremonial.

Ceremonial has not been regarded as characteristic of the Church as reformed, though there are elements of high ceremonial embedded in its system such as the Little Entrance (carrying in of the Bible at the commencement of the service) and the Great Entrance (the carrying in of the sacramental elements). It is true that, even apart from these, the Reformed Church did develop, as any church must, a cultic system, however severe and even un-cultic it must often have appeared to the unsympathetic observer. What has been, not unjustly, charged against her is that the Reformed cult was methodologically restricted. It is easy to understand why. The Reformers rediscovered the prophetic character of the Word of God. This involved the recovery of Biblical faith

and of the sacraments of the Gospel and especially of the
Holy Communion as a true sacrament and not a sacrifice (in
other words as an act of God and not primarily of man). It
implied the remoralizing of religion and much else. These
were boons of a worth so inestimable that at the time no price,
by way of artistic sacrifice, seemed too great to pay.

The result, however, as Kraemer has recently insisted, was
to canalize much of Western public worship and private
devotion within the confines of a too largely verbal culture;
and this, as he rightly says, was in fact un-Biblical. It was
also unrealistic. When Pavlova, asked for the meaning of a
certain dance, replied: ' Do you think I would have danced
it if I could have said it? ' she was making a reply that the
people of the Old Testament world or those in St. Paul's
day would have understood and the eighteenth-century
Puritan would not, for the reason that the Puritan had been
too long and too exclusively inured to a verbal religious culture (utterly vital as that also is for explicit faith and for the
purity of the cult). This limitation inevitably modified
evangelistic and missionary method with the result, it is said,
that the Church—however impressive her educational and
missionary record—did not on the spiritual level touch the
deeper springs of the African nature. There are evidences
that the charge is not entirely without foundation. Even on
the purely social level, significant rituals have an extremely
important role to play as a means of ' combating community
disintegration '.[1] On the spiritual level they are a very important means of expressing the unity of the Body and so
assisting to maintain its continuity. The Sacrament of the
Lord's Supper is of course the supreme instance of this.

Fortunately, in addition to the Sacraments, the Reformers
made another exception to the insistence upon the human
word as the vehicle of the Divine Word, and that exception

[1] *Vide* E. B. Koenker, *The Liturgical Renaissance in the Roman
Catholic Church* (U.S.A., 1954), p. 42.

was deeply significant. While in practice they restricted ritual and, like Calvin, ' made a breach in the holy pictures ', at this point they made a breach in their own verbal and highly intellectualized culture. They opened the mouths of the people who had been mostly silent in the place of worship for something like a thousand years. They permitted the liturgical song—the Scriptural psalms (rendered into metre) and canticles likewise (though it is not certain that these were much used in Scotland except possibly in the royal chapel), followed in course of time by Scriptural paraphrases, hymns, motets, and other sung parts of the service.

## II. RESPONSE TO REVELATION

This development, though in some branches of the Church it has not yet been fully implemented, was providential. The human reaction to God's revelation of himself is, in God's own providence, very varied. Response to God takes as many forms as there are aspects of man's nature, and any cultic system which is to be adequate must include them all. If it omits any, it is wise not to omit the people's music. Faith's fervour demands a song.

The response to revelation—this is what the Bible is about. ' The Veil of the Temple was rent in twain! '—and what then; what on the human side? Different men respond differently, according to temperament and capacity, to the experience of encounter. When the seer encounters God, the mental precipitate (as we previously noted) is an *image*— for instance the thought of God as Judge, Redeemer, Father. When the thinker attempts to rationalize the images into a system, the result is a series of abstract propositions, a *theology* (still much mixed with picture thinking). When the simple believer meets God in the midst of the world, the precipitate of encounter with God is an *action*, a girding with a towel to repeat, in some sort, Christ's life.

But before all this and including all this, when men encounter God redeemingly, the readiest and perhaps the veriest response is *a song*. And since it is doubt (occasioned by sin as doubt is) that is 'our modern crown of thorns', the keynote of the exultation will be that this is primarily a believing and adoring song; it is characteristically a *Te Deum. Cantare amantis est*, which might be translated 'a lover cannot help singing'.

It is not surprising then that this—the Word followed by the song—is the order that appears to have controlled the acts of worship, the devotions and vigils, during the early centuries—first the Word, then the Church's song, and then the prayers; and though in a later century St. John Chrysostom says: 'First prayer and then the Word', this does not alter the basic arrangement. The song follows as the response to the Word. This seems to be not the only but the first characteristic relation of the song to the Word. It is the adoring response.

In practice this order has been subject to some dislocation and, as a result, the music has suffered deterioration; and this has occurred throughout the Church's history and in all her branches.

No doubt the average worshipper has given little thought to the matter. Music in church is one of the things he takes for granted. He has his own favourite hymns, canticles, organ voluntaries, and the like. He is pleased if these are chosen, less happy if they are not. In other words he tends to apply to the selection of music for worship much the same norm as he applies to his choice of a gramophone record at home. He approves or not according to whether or not he 'likes it'. As to what is sung in church, he will certainly expect to find the name of God in the words, because he understands language and in that field is aware of what he is saying. But in the same hymn you may find him quite innocently asking in effect that Pan (or Pandemonium) be in the music, because in this field he is not aware of what he is doing.[1]

Here we see raised in its most stubborn shape and at its most important locus—the person of the ordinary worshipper —a problem that always has been involved for the Church as soon as she uses the arts in worship. The ordinary worshipper, the moment he sings, is at that point and for the time being an artist. He may be a very good or an extremely bad artist, but artist he is; and localized in him, in an acute form, lies the problem of the relationship of Christ to a prevailing culture.

What in specific terms is the issue so far as the music of the Church is concerned? In its simplest form it was stated by Augustine of Hippo in a classic passage on the delights of the ear: [2]

. . . at one time I seem to myself to give them [the church melodies] more honour than is seemly, feeling our minds to be more holily and fervently raised unto a flame of devotion, by the holy words themselves when thus sung, than when not; and that the several affections of our spirit [the suggestion here seems to be of natural emotions] by a sweet variety, have their own proper measures in the voice and singing, by some secret familiarity and sympathy wherewith they are stirred up. But this contentment of the flesh, to which the soul must not be given over to be enervated, doth oft beguile me . . .

In modern parlance what Augustine is saying is that the senses take control and lead the rational faculties by the nose! At other times, thus warned, he goes on to say he would cheerfully have music banned from the devotions, or at least:

that mode seems to me safer, which I remember to have been often told me of Athanasius, Bishop of Alexandria, who made

[1] On this subject, see C. H. H. Parry, *Style in Musical Art* (London, 1911).
[2] *Confessions*, Bk. 9, xxxiii.

the reader of the psalm utter it with so slight inflection of voice, that it was nearer speaking than singing. Yet again, when I remember the tears I shed at the Psalmody of Thy Church, in the beginning of my recovered faith; and how, at the time, I am moved, not with the singing, but with the things sung, when they are sung with a clear voice and suitable modulation, I acknowledge the great use of this institution. Thus I fluctuate between peril of pleasure and experience of profit; inclined the rather (though not as pronouncing an irrevocable opinion) to approve the usage of singing in the church; that so, by the delight of the ears, the weaker minds may rise to the feeling of devotion. Yet when it befalls me to be more moved with the voice than with the words sung, I confess to have sinned, and then had rather not hear music . . .

How Augustine's devotions would have survived the outrage upon the senses and the reason alike of the larger parish church organs of today when ill-advisedly handled, let alone the musical accompaniments of twentieth-century mass-evangelism, is a question fortunately beyond our province. Yet this extreme instance—of mass-music—poses in an acute form the selfsame question that Augustine asked and with which every church-musician and every minister must tax both his conscience and his sense of good taste: What is the office of this subtle, potent, and nowadays all-pervasive accompaniment of worship, this music which converts a simple poem into a divine song or a spiritual offence?

III. A SOLUTION BY WAY OF FUNCTION

It is as well to note in passing that if this is part, however small a part, of the larger problem of the relationship of Christ to the existing culture, this kind of problem cannot be solved by laying down the law, either in the typical Roman way of decretals or by acts of General Assembly. The only solution that controls without destroying the spontaneity of the song is an existential one.

This is the lesson that history points out. In the sixth century Gregory banned the people's musical participation in the services of the Church and thus turned the Church's song virtually into a monkish preserve for well-nigh a millennium. Such a 'reform' was not merely too sweeping; it was utterly mistaken in principle. The Celtic Church chose the better part with its full flood of psalm-singing (a course of twelve for major offices) with congregational responses and collects in between. The Council of Trent in the sixteenth century reformed the music without abandoning the long-accepted principle of excluding the voice of the people. The enactments of the Consistory at Geneva, relatively austere as they were, gave the impression of conceding a point to a popular demand rather than in acknowledging a divine gift; it allowed melody but forbade any enrichment of the musical texture by harmony. As a result Louis Bourgeois had to take his four-part settings of the metrical psalms elsewhere for publication. In fairness it must be added that, remembering Augustine, the position of the Consistory was understandable; if the French Court had itself long been singing such harmonized settings, it had done so for musical pleasure rather than for devotion. Nevertheless the restriction on musical invention appears, by modern standards, to have been too severe.

In every instance, and the list could be extended, reform or control either of the music or of the musicians was urgently called for. Yet, almost always, either the reform was too sweeping or some essential part of the issue at stake eluded the reformers.

The solution then of this species of problem can only be a fluid or 'existential' one. This is another way of saying that the music of faith ought not to be regarded as a problem to be solved, but as a gift of God to be wisely managed.

What is the principle of management? The answer is not in doubt. Music provides, so to speak, wings to faith for the Church in its corporate worship; it helps to interpret the Word and also the better to express man's words. And whatever it does immediately, it does so ultimately and always as the servant of the liturgy, as an instrument strictly harnessed to the liturgical structure in the main offices of the Church.

This, at the Church's best, has always been the office of her music. It was natural at morning prayer to sing the psalm: 'O God, thou art my God; early will I seek thee' and at evening worship: 'Let my prayer be set forth before thee as incense and the lifting up of my hands as the evening sacrifice.' At baptism psalms were always chosen for this fitness of application. 'At the baptism of Cadoc, who founded the church of Cambuslang, the responsory sung by Meuthi, who baptized him, was, "There is a river, the rushing of whose stream maketh glad the city of our God." '[1] And every baptismal office in every branch of the Church indicates the same thing. Sometimes indeed the application is somewhat forced, as if all that is necessary in a psalm is that it should contain a reference to water. Even so, this only serves to underline the point. It was in this way, among others, that the integrity of the service, both as to sense and artistic quality, was maintained.

This integrity requires always to be safeguarded by knowledge and thought. Hymns, which are after all the typical liturgical song of the churches of the Reformation in modern times, have been chosen by the clergy for a variety of reasons and from a variety of motives other than the one that is essential. They have been used as a 'softening-up' process before the all-important sermon (as if the music of the Church were nothing more than a means of 'conditioning the dog to beg'); or because a particular hymn is a favourite of Miss So-and-So who has specially requested it and who—

[1] Duncan Macgregor, op. cit., p. 24.

the minister is in no danger of forgetting—contributes generously to the funds of the church; or because the minister thinks a particular hymn or anthem will 'create atmosphere'; or because the tune is popular and 'good-going'.

On a rather higher level of purpose the complete list of items sung throughout a service has sometimes been chosen to reinforce the message of the sermon. It is true that the 'office hymn' may fittingly strike the key-note of a festival or other service, either at the beginning or between the lections and the sermon, as at once a devotional interpretation and a response. Nevertheless any one sermon reflects only a fragment of Christian truth. Therefore a service in which this note alone is struck throughout the sung service has clearly sacrificed balance and completeness.

If the new concern about worship throughout the churches does nothing else, it will have served the Church well by putting the hymn in its true place and keeping it there by restoring its liturgical function within the structure of the service. This will restore continuity to the various parts of the service, integrity and cumulative significance to the whole. Incidentally when the policy of the Roman Church was revised in recent times, it was laid down that the people were permitted to sing hymns which 'correspond to the various parts of the Mass'.[1] Here the same principle was recognized.

## IV. THE STRUCTURAL PATTERN

This implies that we must look at the classic pattern which basically has been common to every branch of the Church, whether Eastern, Gallican, Roman, or Scotican. In its matured shape the first part of the service preceding the reading and preaching of the Word of God is the Humble Approach in acknowledgement of God as Creator and of

[1] J. A. Jungmann, S.J., *Public Worship* (New York, 1941), p. 44.

ourselves as creatures. The characteristic note here, in many ancient liturgies, is struck by an introit psalm, and as everyone knows, the typical attitude of the psalms is acknowledgement of God and of his mighty power and works; and this is followed by the people's *Kyries*—'Lord have mercy', acknowledging our creatureliness. Both these notes are present in one action in the *Gloria in excelsis Deo* (one of the Western Church's many debts to the Eastern Church). Any singing at this part of the service ought to be to words along these lines if not in these specific terms, either first by the people themselves or, if these prayers have first been offered on their behalf by the minister, as a kind of liturgical echo or response on the people's part. This is not as yet the place for adoration through either prayer or praise, as we shall see.

The second part of the service—still part of the so-called 'liturgy of the catechumens' or 'liturgy of the Word'—comprises the Word of God in lections and sermon. Here too any singing ought either to echo the theme or to be in the nature of a liturgical response to it. From an early date the *gradual*[1] *psalm* (the earliest chant in the Christian service, inherited from the synagogue) stood between the Epistle and the Gospel and appears to have been selected, certainly on great days, to reflect the tone or message of the Scripture lesson.[2] This is as it ought to be. The song connected with the Word of God read and preached should be a liturgical echo or response.

In the third great action of the service, that which follows the Word of God, namely the Communion (the Liturgy of the faithful, otherwise called the Liturgy of the Upper

[1] So called from the *gradus* (steps) of the altar or of the *ambo* from which the lesson was read, or possibly because the psalm was sung from the sanctuary steps in earlier time by a soloist.

[2] Dix, op. cit., p. 39, mentions, in the Roman use possibly as early as the second century, the singing of Psalm 90, vv. 1-12, following the reading of Hosea 6, at the Paschal vigil.

Room), almost universally the classical acts of liturgical response are: first, the *Nicene Creed*: secondly, after the sermon, preface, and other words according to the particular use, the *Ter-Sanctus* with *Benedictus*,[1] and the *Agnus Dei*.[2]

This, as we noted earlier, is what we expect to find as the response to the Word that redeems—a believing *adoration* and with it (since these two notes are never separated in any genuine experience of God) its converse in loving creaturely humility.

Now an interesting and also significant point arises. This, after the Word, is not entirely unlike the pattern and mood which marks the opening part of the service before the Word is read and preached—the initial humble acknowledgement of God the Creator and of ourselves as creatures.

There is however a significant difference which ought to be reflected in the prayers and in the music. It is that if the earlier prayers are reverential, the later ones are adoring, and the reason is clear. The later prayers and praises, since they follow the Word of God, are for that very reason enlightened and uplifted in a high and holy exaltation to a degree that the earlier ones are not.

It is true that the service as a whole is that of the redeemed community, and it would be ridiculous to suggest that the earlier prayers are unenlightened. It is true also that it is Christ, by his Holy Spirit, who prays in and through his Church, not merely as a collection of individuals but as his Body. Nevertheless the individuals who are of that Body have come to the weekly office of worship in some degree stained by the soil of life and blinded by the world's false values. For the fuller refreshing of vision they must await

[1] 'Holy, holy, holy, Lord God of Hosts, Heaven and earth are full of Thy glory: Glory be to Thee, O God most High, Blessed is He that cometh in the name of the Lord: Hosanna in the highest.'

[2] 'Lamb of God that takest away the sins of the world, have mercy upon us, etc.'

the renewed inbreak of the Eternal Word. Once more—for the prayer of the Body is the perpetual recapitulation of the ' salvation events '—the veil must be ' rent in twain '. Therefore the prayers that follow the sermon are enlightened prayers to a degree that the earlier reverential prayers could not attain.

This may also explain why the note of submission is repeated also *after* the Word of God in the ' *Lamb of God . . . have mercy upon us . . .* ' Confession of creatureliness, and then of sinfulness, is indeed made, and rightly made, early in the service, and ought to be followed by an absolution or Scriptural declaration of God's pardon. Indeed it is God's forgiveness, declared at this point, that makes it possible for the hearer to ' hear the Word of God ' at all, or at least properly to hear it, not merely as judgement but as mercy, favour, and gracious promise. In the same way it is God's forgiveness, sealed in his Word, that makes a true repentance possible. Thus in the classical prayers, even the ' Lamb of God that takest away the sins of the world, have mercy upon us ' after the sermon expresses a more enlightened repentance than the ' Lord have mercy ' before it.

If this distinction which we have drawn be acknowledged, it will be seen to control also the musical settings used for the Church's service, whether they be ' service music ' in the strict traditional sense—that is, the setting of the different parts of the Holy Communion—or simply the hymns, psalms, and anthems used in the ordinary parish church on occasions of non-sacramental worship.

Consider some of the forms or formulas which enjoy a regular residence within the threshold of worship. Going through them everyone feels the difference between the words that are already winged and require only music to make them soar, and those that are relatively pedestrian. The *Apostles' Creed*, whether it be regarded as (what originally it was) a baptismal formula, a deposit of belief or merely a declaration of allegiance, achieves a kind of monolithic dignity by its very sparseness of utterance within its obviously limited intention. As between the *Apostles' Creed*, however, and the winged utterance of the *Te Deum* (the petitionary verses at the end are a later addition to the original and fall into a different category) it is the *Te Deum* that sings itself into the heart, and from the heart to the Throne, where one may not readily imagine the 'angels and archangels and all the company of heaven' saying the *Apostles' Creed*, but can with no great stress of imagination hear them singing, even in heaven, the ever-soaring: 'We praise Thee, O God, we acknowledge Thee to be the Lord . . .' as indeed one can imagine them singing any one of the resplendent adorations that St. John of Patmos in his vision heard rising to the Throne.

After the Word of God read and preached, the Church's characteristic song will thus be enlightened and exalted adoration. The note to be sounded will be the kind of note that is heard in the Sanctus ('Holy, holy, holy . . .') or the *Te Deum* (which of course includes the *Sanctus*). Though the service be one of non-eucharistic parish worship for people who will in any case not communicate that day, as in a Scottish forenoon service or the Anglican Matins, the rule ought to be the same; there should be the same type of enlightened and adoring response to the Word of God as the *Sanctus* provides in the Communion Office.

This too can quite as well be expressed in the form of a hymn for all to sing as in that of a canticle or anthem by skilled singers. It is the response of the whole Church to the Word. The Reformers were soundly interpreting the Biblical theology when they insisted that the song of the Church was to be liturgical song, no mere privilege of a selected corps of singers, but that of the whole Body. Fortunately the Church is not entirely lacking in hymns, accessible to the people's attainments, and marked by this objective, traditional, yet deeply personal quality of adoring acknowledgement and gratitude.[1] Nevertheless it is also much to be desired that the best of our composers of church music should provide us with settings of the canticles,[2] the *Sanctus*, *Gloria in excelsis*, *Trisagion*, and some of the Scriptural adorations, in a music sufficiently noble in expression and at the same time not beyond the capacity of average congregations to learn.

This is important, it may even be utterly vital, not indeed for 'brighter services', but for that recovery of worship which is the true splendour of the Church and is, beyond all others, the great need of our day. For it is here, at this point of the service—even where there is no Holy Communion in the sacramental mode—that there rises the climax, the Church's response to the Word of God, before it offers itself to God in self-oblation and girds itself to the ministry of intercession.[3]

So much for the pattern.

## V. THE ART OF SELECTION

Thus far we have considered the principle of arrangement, the high and low points in the spiritual graph. But what of the principle of selection—of the music itself? Why is a setting of a psalm by one composer nobly appropriate while that by another is not, however much it may appeal to what

[1] 'We praise, we worship Thee, O God' (from Philip Gell's *Psalms and Hymns*, 1815) is a short metrical version of the *Te Deum*. 'Round the Lord in glory seated' is built on the theme of the *Sanctus*, as is Heber's 'Holy, holy, holy, Lord God Almighty' and Tersteegen's 'God reveals His presence'. Yet others include the *Sanctus* idea; and very many are instinct with this note of pure adoration.

[2] And especially the *Te Deum* in the original short version, since the inspiration of composers seldom seems adequate to sustain itself throughout the extended—surely for modern use over-extended—version which is normally used.

[3] *Vide* Appendix.

H

Augustine called 'the affections'? The middle of the twentieth century witnessed a fresh crop of experiments, the new rhythmic emphasis of Father Gelineau's psalm-settings and the concession to 'popular' taste of Geoffrey Beaumont's *Folk Mass*. Experiments such as these are intended to build a viable road on which unaccustomed feet may find their way to the place of worship and the stumbling-blocks of the old pointings of prose psalm chants may be removed so that regular worshippers may participate intelligently. How is the minister or musician to know what to use and what to avoid?

If a revolution is, even partly, 'an appeal from a lower to a higher tradition', a salutary revolution in this field cannot take place without at least a general knowledge of the traditions.

First, then, neither the minister nor the organist will be able to deal competently with the selection of the music unless he is aware of the Church's inheritance from all the Christian ages. They come to us, these long ages, full-handed, rich in musical idiom, and, it would not be too much to say, each with its own contribution to the economy of worship. Here is Hebrew cantillation (not for ordinary use but service-able as incidental music for Biblical drama still). Here is the pentatonic scale of folk-music, baptized again into the service of the Church in our time. Here are the speech-rhythms of the Church's chant, hallowed by immemorial use, in the Gregorian melodies and tones. Here is the rich but delicate texture of Tudor polyphony and its contemporary, the service-settings of Palestrina, of which that deeply sensitive critic, Robert Bridges, said that it was almost as if the sacred words had become musical. Here is the solemn, evocative metrical psalmody of Geneva and Scotland and the charac-teristic chorale of Germany (music which is essentially melo-dic, traditionally sung in unison, and strong by virtue of its economy of line). Here is the somewhat uncritical exuber-

ance of the eighteenth century, the 'century of divine songs'
(and of many not so divine), the sentiment of the nineteenth-
century Anglican hymn-tune composers, and the clean austere writing of the best of the modern church composers.

Here, to put it in another way, is catholicity, the true
inclusive catholicity which repudiates all that is merely
sectional and sectarian; a well-compiled hymn-book is indeed
the most ecumenical book in the world, the Bible alone
excepted. Through the mystery of the Church's liturgical
song, Europe and America—the lands of the great wheels of
industry, representatives of this frightened and frightening
race of men who have plumbed the abysses of the ocean and
annihilated the spaces as if they would displenish the very
planets, and who in the same moment dread the powers they
have unleashed—this pioneer race, or at least the believers
from among it, join hands in devotion with the Pilgrim
Fathers, with the men of Geneva and Worms, with the
Cistercians, in the days of their first fervour, singing their
plain-chants, as someone described it, 'lovingly', with the
Celtic and Gallican churches (a special part this of the Scottish Christian inheritance), with Ambrose, with the first
Christians at Antioch, with the synagogue, and with the
Upper Room itself.

This, no less, is the heritage which the Christian ages bring
to us. In the fulness of the Church's song one is borne on the
full stream of Christian thought and experience in all centuries, and can hear, in the echoes of the music from our
Lord's time until now, 'one generation crying to another'.
Ours is a generation in which people sorely require a
refreshed sense of the long ages of God, of God's slow finger
in history and of his awesome patience with the sons and
daughters of men; and here, within the covers of any good
hymn-book (to go no further), it is all brought vividly home
by way of the senses.

How much of it is both usable and worthy of its function?

Clearly not all that is technically within the average worshipper's capacity is spiritually adequate for the purposes of common worship as we have tried in these chapters to define them. This rules out a great mass of popular but unworthy music. The suitable music that is left will be a music, to quote Robert Bridges,[1] ' different from what is heard elsewhere . . . a sacred music, devoted to its purpos, a music whose peace should still passion, whose dignity should strengthen our faith . . . a music worthy of the fair temples in which we meet and of the holy words of our liturgy; a music whose expression of the mystery of things unseen never allow'd any trifling motiv to ruffle the sanctity of its reserve '.

A prescription such as this does not limit the field nearly so drastically as is generally thought; indeed it is only a prevalent ignorance of what is available that has caused people to harbour the notion that the choice is between what is popular and what is good; for this is not the choice. Some of the music that is beautifully fitting for worship is quite certainly beyond the capacity of the ordinary member of the Church. There remains none the less a more than sufficiently large corpus of hymns, psalms, canticles, and other service music, bearing the stamp of fitness desiderated by Dr. Bridges, yet well within the powers both of performance and of enjoyment of the average congregation.

Discrimination and sympathy are necessary if the Church's music is to be wisely chosen. If it is right, as it surely is, that the congregation should take their full part in the Church's praise, then the means must be supplied for them to do so by choosing music within their compass. While the primary object of all church singing is to ' glorify God ', this cannot be properly done unless the music is such as also to ' unite the Body ' in the shape of the assembled congregation. This

[1] R. Bridges, *Collected Essays*, xxi-xxvi (London, 1935), p. 65. In the quotation Bridges' own spelling is retained.

does not, however, imply the lowest quality of tunes to suit the lowest taste present. It is sometimes forgotten that tunes which are blatant, arrogant, or sentimental are quite as likely to exclude one part of the Body, as tunes that are impossibly 'high-brow' are likely to exclude the rest. In neither class of tunes is to be found the music of common worship. Such music must be on the one hand sufficiently accessible to popular capacity to be sung with fervour and understanding, and at the same time sufficiently pure to make it seem 'almost as if the sacred words had become musical'.

## VI. SOCIOLOGICAL FACTORS

An additional guide to wise discrimination will be found in a consideration to which a good deal of attention has been directed in the field of historical theology but not very much in that of church music. If it is sometimes the nature of heresy to overstate a neglected truth and at other times to neglect some truth that is vital, then every generation tends towards some heresy, and its arts will reflect the error, just as the cherished art of previous ages may tend to correct it. Certainly an art is frequently a sounding-board for a community's philosophy, its attitudes to life and its religious doctrines. The furnishings of the early basilican or the later Reformed churches clearly reflected a sacramental theology different from that of the medieval Roman structures; and indeed it is difficult to believe that the renewal of interest in the 'basilican posture',[1] does not indicate or herald a shifting of the theological emphasis.

What has this to do with the music of the Church? Surely much. Reinhold Niebuhr in the opening paragraph of his *Faith and History*[2] pointed out that though on any grounds life for the people of the twentieth century would have been

[1] I.e. the celebrant standing behind the Holy Table.
[2] London, 1949.

hazardous and their problems difficult, the difficulty, both moral and political, was 'the more dangerous because the men of this generation had to face the rigours of life in the twentieth century with nothing but the soft illusions of the previous two centuries to cover their spiritual nakedness. There was nothing in the creeds and dogmas of these centuries which would have enabled modern men either to anticipate or to understand the true nature of the terrors and tumults to which they would be exposed.'

The now thoroughly discredited optimism of those years managed to maintain itself into the twentieth century only because it embraced a good deal of sentimentality, the attitude of mind, that is to say, which prefers to ignore inconvenient factors. It is to be expected that such an attitude should be reflected not only in literature and sermons but in popular music such as hymns. Anyone who cares to play over on the piano (even without following the marks of expression which themselves were significant of the sentimental approach of the older hymn-books) a hymn-tune by John Bacchus Dykes[1] or Joseph Barnby, will recognize the characteristic idiom and flavour of a still dominant type of popular hymnody. This was the song of a church that had drunk deeply of that sentimental optimism which Niebuhr rightly indicts, and which was characteristic of it.

The ancestry of this trend is complicated. There is a network of collateral relationships which warn of the danger of over-simplification in analysis. Nevertheless certain stages can be discerned which affected the field of the Church's music.

Descartes has been credited with the responsibility for driving the Western soul in on itself in a novel degree of

[1] Excepting his *Nicaea*, which owes its strength neither to Dykes nor to his century but to the 'king of chorales', namely 'Sleepers wake', a piece written and composed during a devastating plague about 1597-8, by a pastor who had sometimes to conduct thirty funerals a day.

self-consciousness by his *cogito ergo sum* (' I think, therefore I am ') though, like most who have given their name to a system, his genius lay in developing something which was in the air at the time. The new trend in philosophy was symtomatic of much that was also to happen in the field of faith. Puritan man, confronted first by the contradiction between the newly discovered Bible and the old discredited Church, and later by the conflicting interpretations of Scripture offered by Independency, was driven to seek a corroborative warrant for assurance of salvation interiorly, and ultimately in the form of compelling emotional assurance. From this point the subjective and emotional can be traced, growing ever more pronounced, producing its flower in the great romantics, and some of its weeds in the hymnody of all branches of the Church.

This trend and its significance cannot be mistaken. As the emphasis on personal emotion grew stronger, the idea of the Church as the Body of Christ weakened, although at the same time, as if in compensation, Christians became more gregarious, which is not the same thing as being the Body of Christ. No one who is musically versed can play and sing a metrical psalm or a theologically controlled hymn set to a Genevan Reformation tune, and compare it to William Cowper's 'O for a closer walk with God' to the tune *Martyrdom*, without feeling the difference between the nobly objective common song of the whole Body at worship and the individualistic and subjective utterance of the later hymn (both words and tune) which breaks the Body up into a collection of persons each at his private prayers. In the same way no one can play and sing Nicolai's strongly serene chorale 'Sleepers wake' and compare it with the general run of the productions of German pietism a century and a half later without discerning that in the latter there is already a certain loss both of artistic and spiritual bone.

It is perhaps necessary to issue a warning in passing that it is hardly possible properly to assess the effect which is here being discussed from an examination of those of the eighteenth-century hymn-tunes which are still to be found in considerable numbers in our standard hymn-books, since the blatantly florid features with which musicians decorated (or rather defaced) the tunes have been mostly pruned away; modern editors have in fact made reasonably honest tunes of them.

Study the great hymn-books, then, and it becomes clear that the thoughts, the strengths and weaknesses of the passing generations have stamped themselves upon the pages. One will find in them the passion-cleansed, God-conscious plain-songs, the strong objective psalmody of the Reformation, the beginnings of decline already hinted at in the early Puritans, and a failure to control that gravitational movement described by Miss Underhill when she writes: 'The tendency of all worship to decline from adoration to demand, and from the supernatural to the ethical, shows how strong a pull is needed to neutralize the anthropocentric trend of the human mind . . .'[1] One will also find in a hymn-book most of the other representative figures of the passing years, the humanists, the humanitarians, the optimists, and the liberal theologians. If we choose them and use them, as we are free to do, we ought at least to know what it is we are doing and accept responsibility.

Here too however are ancient and abiding landmarks. Isaac Watts represents the Calvinist strain, strong and austere because it is Scriptural. The Wesleys represent the Lutheran strain, also Scriptural but less obviously dogmatic and emotionally warmer. It will be seen that while hymns at their worst have reflected the errors or refractions of the thought of an era, the best hymns have at different times been instrumental in maintaining a full and true conception

[1] Evelyn Underhill, *Worship* (London, 1943 ed.), cn. i, p. 17.

of the Gospel which was otherwise imperilled by distortion or in danger of neglect.

Hymns can be potent instruments both of revision and of recall. It was in reaction to an evangelicalism that had grown too individualistic and subjective that the Tractarians felt called upon to reassert a doctrine of the Church. And here surely is a warning and a challenge. Newman himself spoke of the surprise that 'from beginnings so small' so great a movement should develop so swiftly. In view of the characteristic fervour of the evangelicalism of the eighteenth century, it must have appeared at first as if the Tractarians had little hope of enduring successes. Looking from the more detached standpoint of today we can see that it was precisely by reason of the characteristic weaknesses of that supposedly dominant evangelicalism that the Anglo-Catholic party found an unexpected degree of hospitality in certain minds, and among them some of the finest of the century. A mere prettiness of vestments could not explain the tidal wave of that new and different fervour. It was by saying the neglected thing that the movement won an unexpected dominance. That neglected thing was the objective thing: the relationship of Gospel and Church, and of Church and individual.

## VII. THE VEXED QUESTION OF OBJECTIVITY

Why this powerful reassertion of emphasis—which has proved to be a persuasive and gathering movement throughout all branches of the Church—upon the objective in worship? The word is bandied about, sometimes without clear recognition of what it signifies. It means very much what W. P. Ker had in mind when he advised writers to 'keep your eye on the object'. In terms of worship it means looking outward to God rather than inward to ourselves.

It is sometimes held in criticism of forms of worship which are 'objective' that they are necessarily lacking in emotional warmth. Let us notice then the ascending scale of objective worship from the factual base to the pinnacle of song.

First, the basic objectivity in worship is solidly ontological, if the term may be used without becoming involved in the classic philosophic debate to which its use sometimes gives rise. It implies that worship depends not first on psychological considerations nor even on those that are ethical but moves in a world of objective persons and facts, in which the distinction between natural and supernatural is seen to be no necessary antithesis but a relationship subsisting in the being of God himself. Indeed it is significant that it is in the great eucharistic prayer that some early liturgies elaborate the idea of God's glory as manifested in the Creation, glorying in 'the earth and all that is therein, the sea, the fountains, the rivers, the lakes and all things that are in them . . .'[1] This prepares for the *Sanctus*. Such prayer is as healthily objective as the brusque acceptance of the given creation by a certain Scottish divine.[2] Pointing to a bird while on a country walk with a friend, he remarked: 'There's a woodcock', to be met with the disdainful: 'That's not *my* idea of a woodcock!'; to which the minister replied: 'No? But it's God's!' This is as solidly Biblical as the majestic acceptance of facts by the writers of the Book of Genesis who do not dream of suggesting that the Creation is good because man happens to approve of it; it is good because God says it is good, and that is that.

Room for philosophical criticism there must be even in the life of faith; it is one of the means by which faith, matched against everything that is hostile to itself, comes into its own as faith. But in the act of worship, no. Here is the acceptance of the objective reality of God as the ground of all that is and will be.

---

[1] *Anaphora of St. Mark*, quoted by E. Underhill, op. cit., p. 113.
[2] Said to be A. K. H. Boyd; *vide* Dr. John Baillie's *The Sense of the Presence of God* (1962), p. 191. The story is also told of Dr. John Ker.

It is essential that our hymnody should strike this note.

Secondly, there is what might be described as objectivity in worship because worship is not primarily a matter of subjective emotion but an action, a traffic of God and man. This too is the note of the earlier services, where the idea of the *Maranatha* ('Lord, come!') still operated as a sanction in the interests of purity, and the ancient 'fencing' word was spoken: 'If any man be holy, let him come; if any man be not, let him repent.' This is personal but it is not subjective. It is not self-examination, it is a call to be examined by God. This is a traffic of persons, with the eyes and the emphasis on the Other Person.

And thirdly, there is even what may not improperly be called objectivity in the emotional concomitants of worship. That there is a place, and a large place, for emotional warmth in worship ought to be admitted. It is however important to know what that place is, and to recognize that a genuine emotion towards God cannot be engineered by the manipulation of worship-modes, though certain types of hymn will without difficulty liberate something of the unharnessed natural emotion that is latent in every worshipper, and this may readily pass as emotion towards God.

While it is true that 'a lover cannot but sing' (*cantare amantis est*), there are two themes that the lover may celebrate in his song. He may celebrate his own emotions or he may celebrate the beauties and graces of his beloved. The one song is subjective, the other finely and healthily objective.[1]

The parallel in the Church's song is exact. Once it is drawn, everyone recognizes the difference between the hymns of William Cowper celebrating his own despairing emotions—

[1] Subjectivity and objectivity are both expressed in Kierkegaard's 'God looked upon me in my conscience, and now it is impossible for me to forget that he sees me. And because God looked upon me I had and have to look towards God.' *Journals* (1847) (ed. and trans. by A. Dru, Princeton and London, 1938), p. 211.

' where is the blessedness I knew? '—and the serene objective song of the *Nunc dimittis:* ' Lord, now lettest thou thy servant depart in peace according to thy Word, for mine eyes have beheld thy salvation ', or of the psalms which rest in God's power and glory.

VIII. SUMMING UP

The question is not first whether the music we employ for the people's song in church shall be of good quality or bad. That question arises secondarily under the discussion as to what kind of music will be capable of serving the purposes of worship in general and of that particular act of worship at which a piece of music is to be used. In other words, a sung item in the service ought either to constitute some part of it, or to echo the word already spoken, functioning in fact as the people's liturgical response. It is natural at the commencement of the service to sing, for example, Psalm 95: ' Come, let us worship and bow down, let us kneel before the Lord our Maker . . .'; or to sing in association with the lessons and sermon either a hymn such as Wesley's ' Come Holy Ghost our souls inspire . . . unseal the Holy Book ' or an ' office hymn '; to sing, after the Word of God has been read and preached, a pure and believing adoration such as the *Te Deum* or a hymn like ' God reveals His presence '; and to close with a dismissal hymn, with one in praise of Christ, or with an exultant recollection of the Communion of Saints.

Such a function—to act as the servant of the liturgy—will require music of many different kinds, serene or jubilant as the occasion may demand. Yet there will always be upon it a restraint, the restraint imposed by reverence. Public music, as C. H. H. Parry (I think) has said, tends to blatancy, private music to intimacy (or, in cruder terms, to ' palliness '). The true song of the Church is in neither of these categories. It is simply a music that is *real for its purpose*. It will sound—

we repeat once again—'almost as if the sacred words had become musical'.

So far as hymns are concerned, this purpose will require the use, not indeed exclusively but very largely, of those sections of a hymn-book that deal with God in creation and providence; with our Lord Jesus Christ, his life, example, passion, death, resurrection, exaltation, intercession, and his praise: with the Holy Spirit, the Church, the Communion of Saints; with the Sacraments; with morning and evening worship—in short with the whole corpus of the Church's teaching in association with the offices of the Church. In these sections of any good hymn-manual are to be found the bulk of the great objective hymns, which include also the noblest hymns of the Church.

What we have attempted to say here about hymns applies equally to motets, canticle settings, and other service music, though for obvious reasons the risk of general debasement is not so great in this field as in that of hymnody.

We have no right to claim different standards for the music of the Church than discerning minds would claim for the products of any other branch of art. 'For—believe me, Gentlemen' (Quiller Couch lectured to his students) '—so far as Handel stands above Chopin, as Velasquez above Greuze, even so far stand the great masculine objective writers above all who appeal to you by parade of personality or private sentiment.'

'Mention of these great masculine "objective" writers', he goes on, 'brings me to my last word: which is, "Steep yourselves in *them:* habitually bring all to the test of *them:* for while you cannot escape the fate of all style, which is to be personal, the more of catholic manhood you inherit from those great loins the more you will assuredly beget." '[1]

No less than in the matter of writing good prose should

[1] 'Lecture on Style', in *On the Art of Writing* (Cambridge, 1916), p. 165.

it be said: Steep yourselves also in the great liturgical tradition which, the more positive it is, absorbed in the Birth, the Passion, and the Mighty Acts, is to that extent the more intimate and tender.

And since the service is one and indivisible, no less in music than in liturgical fulness and fitness of expression, the attempt should be made to understand where to look for those modes which, so far as humanly contrived modes can ever be, are fitted for the worship of God; lest our way of offering our song to God be not, as is sometimes claimed, all that our people can manage, but instead is simply, as Robert Bridges asserted, 'an uncorrected bad habit'.

# CHAPTER FIVE

# THE MOUTH-PIECE

---

You may do what you like, mankind will believe no one but God; and he only can persuade mankind who believes that God has spoken to him. No one can give faith unless he has faith; the persuaded persuade, as the indulgent disarm. JOUBERT, quoted by MATTHEW ARNOLD: *Critical Essays*, loc. cit.

## I. THE SERMON AS THE OCCASION OF ENCOUNTER

We have now discussed the vagrant Word of God abroad in the world (as the wind 'bloweth where it listeth'), the Word as canalized in the liturgies, as crystallized in the image and as winged in the people's religious song. But what of the personal mouth-piece of the Word, the man who preaches and leads the people's prayers?

To speak of the Word of God implies, in the spiritual sense, a hearer; does it also imply, in the literal sense, a preacher? The question may be expressed thus: What is it that marks the difference—a difference that everybody feels—between a good theological essay and a good sermon? Why, instead of having in our churches a lectern and a pulpit, do we not bid people open their Bibles and read silently for themselves and then, having distributed a printed exposition by some reliable expositor, bid them read and ponder it?

We all know the answer. It is that a good theological essay is a helpful arrangement and criticism of ideas with a view to better understanding of some objective truth, while a sermon, though it ought to be built on this, is something more, something different. It is a going into action.

Even outside the field of religious experience, everyone

feels the difference between being left to read for himself and being, as it were, taken in hand by a speaker who is the mouthpiece of a conviction, cause, or party. Here is Lord Rosebery's description of one of the most arresting political orators of his time, William Pitt, afterwards Lord Chatham, as he addressed the House of Commons:

We can fancy him rising in the House which subsides into silence and eager attention. . . . His opening is solemn and impressive. Then he warms to his subject. He states his argument. He recalls matters of history and his own personal recollections. Then with an insinuating wave of his arm his voice changes, and he is found to be drowning some hapless wight with ridicule. Then he seems to ramble a little, he is marking time and collecting himself for what is coming. Suddenly the rich notes swell into the fulness of a great organ, and the audience find themselves borne into the heights of a sublime burst of eloquence. Then he sinks again into a whisper full of menace which carries some cruel sarcasm to some quivering heart. Then he is found playing about his subject, pelting snowballs as he proceeds. . . . So all through the speech men sit as though paralysed. . . . He will not finish without some lofty declamation which may be the culminating splendour of the effort. . . . And as he sits down, perhaps with little applause, the tension of nerves, almost agonising in its duration and concentration, snaps like a harpstring; the buzz of animated conversation breaks forth with an ecstasy of relief. The audience disperses still under the spell. . . .[1]

What is the explanation of this power? It lies perhaps hardly at all in the realm of ' personality ', since that can be a cheap, as it often is today a cheapened and a cheapening thing.[2] Partly it lies in the mystery of genius and the power

---

[1] *Chatham: his Early Life and Connections*, ch. XXII, pp. 496 ff.

[2] ' In certain respects the preacher's personality may obscure the very message it wings, just as a magical Sacrament may in another way. There may easily be too much of his sermon and too little of Christ's

of natural yet sublime passion to kindle others. This how-ever all must agree, that such speaking is a going into action. You have the impression of people being dealt with, of people running for shelter, or arguing and excusing, or enlisting under some banner. The difference between Chatham's utterance and Christian preaching is that preaching is a sacramental action and the preacher in orders a sacramental person.

Preaching has been described as a 'manifestation of the Incarnate Word, from the written Word, by the spoken word', but it is even more than this. It is the occasion of encounter. It is a man speaking in such a way and under such a direction that the God who is eternal may be heard to utter his solving and saving Word in the situation that is contemporary (and this 'Word' is not to be understood as an intellectual symbol but as a personal action). It is Christ's witness to the Father, using the mind and lips of the preacher in such a way that the Holy Spirit is felt to witness both to Christ and the Father in the mind, heart, and will of the hearer. Definitions may be multiplied endlessly; but which-ever definition be preferred and whatever preaching is con-ceived to be, it is primarily and characteristically this—a personal action and that action God's.

Such is the Biblical preaching. Recall how Amos opened his prophecy by castigating the nations who formed a cruel iron ring round Israel, whipping them, lash upon lash:

'For three transgressions of Damascus, and for four, I will not turn away the punishment thereof . . .' (And here is stated the indictment.)

'For three transgressions of . . . Tyre . . . of Edom . . . of the Ammonites . . . of Moab . . .'

Gospel, too much of his temperament and too little of his message . . . Many churches have come to idolize the gifts of the preacher more than the gift of grace.' (P. T. Forsyth, *The Church and the Sacra-ments* (London, 2nd. ed., 1947), ch. XLI, p. 231.

I

until surely his auditory, their memory scarred by old
oppressions and dreads, cheered the fiery words to the echo;
and then swiftly the blow fell where it was least expected:

'For three transgressions of *Judah* and for four . . . For
three transgressions of *Israel* and for four, I will not turn
away the punishment thereof.'

Almost you can see the shocked, startled faces. Was there
a hearer, one wonders, who did not feel as if he had been
*ambushed*? Whatever else that preaching was, it was a going
into action; and the prophets believed unquestioningly that
it was God's action in the midst of men.

Preaching, however, is only likely to remain uncorrupt,
delivered from idiosyncracy, when it is controlled by a doctrine of the Church.

It is Christ's preaching to his Church and it is also the
Church's prophetic proclamation to the world. Read the
greatest of the preachers, Hugh Latimer in the sixteenth
century, for example, or Eckhart in the fourteenth, and
always this is the feel of it. It is an action and it is action in
the midst of the Church—to the Church and from the
Church. Here is Eckhart on the Epistle of St. James i. 17:

So St. James says 'Every good and perfect gift cometh down
from heaven.' Now notice! You should know that those men
who surrender themselves to God and seek His will alone with
all diligence, whatever God gives to these men, that is the best.
You can be as certain of this as that God lives; it must necessarily be the best, and there could be no other way that could
be better. Even if it should happen that another seemed better,
it would not be so good for you, for God wills this way and
not another way, and this way must necessarily be the best way
for you. . . . Every day in the Paternoster we call out and
exclaim: 'Lord, Thy will be done,' and when His will is done
we are angry and not satisfied with His will. . . .

Where is the introduction? There is none. The exegesis

comes later in the sermon. Eckhart walks right into the fray. When he preaches, God is busy.

Without this conception of the Church and of preaching the minister may utter sermons but he will never preach. The Church herself, static and institutional as she constantly appears to be, is really an ever-continuing action of God. She is certainly not an institutional Ivory Tower into which people wearied of mental fight may creep to find an untroubled salvation. The Church is no less dynamic a fellowship than the Kingdom in the Gospels, where we get the impression of Jesus speaking the word of grace or stretching out the finger of pity and proclaiming: 'See! in the very speaking of this word and in the very movement of compassion—whether men accept the word or not and whether they are healed or not—the Kingdom of God is present!' It is 'extant and actual'! A Church static and institutional, which no longer has this dynamic character, has ceased to be the Church. Thus the *characteristic* functions of the Church are (a) the Sacraments of the Gospel which are not primarily God's gifts of a substance but God's gracious action; even while the consecrated substance is necessary for the action in the same way as there had to be an Incarnation that God might work a redemption; (b) the preaching of the Gospel, which is not primarily the presentation of ideas but God's dealing with men, even though ideas are necessary for the dealing; and (c) the girding with a towel and serving.

## II. ELEMENTS OF TENSION IN THE CONCEPTION OF CHURCH AND OF PREACHER

It is quite easy to affirm these things. And this dynamic conception of the Church has been used to 'let the Church out'. When people point the finger at anything that is not of Christ in the Church as they see it, the reply may be given:

' What you say is true, only *that*—the thing you see is not the real Church; the Church is not institutional but dynamic.'

The fact remains, nevertheless, that the Church is referred to in the New Testament as the Body (which is a visible and tangible thing) and that she appears before the eyes of men as institutional, shaping herself in congregations of actual and not merely ideal people, in dogmas, institutional arrangements, and forms of prayer, in all of which imperfection may appear, and by the frailty of which the Word of God may be made ' of none effect'.

A minister will be advised to face this issue with his congregation, for their good and his own. If he wishes an arresting text, there is one to be found in the way St. Paul addresses the envelope, so to speak, in his first letter to the Corinthian Church. One wonders what thoughts passed through the apostle's mind, knowing what he did of the moral condition of certain groups within that congregation, as he penned the address: ' to the *church of God* . . . which is at *Corinth* . . . sanctified . . . called . . .' The risk St. Paul took in calling this God's Church at Corinth is of course no different from the risk Jesus took in calling Peter and Andrew, and which God took in calling Israel and saying ' Thou art my son . . .' The very facing of this issue will compel a very necessary reassessment of what is meant by being a church. ' It is not enthusiasm, but dogma, that differentiates a Christian from a pagan society ', wrote T. S. Eliot,[1] and the distinction between the Church and the pagan world is precisely the same.

Loosening of the dogmatic structure always marks a weakening of the Church at the most vulnerable, because most characteristic, place in her economy. Before the Church is anything else at all, she is a believing community. It was characteristic of the period of decline during which the humanists had their way that the word ' Shibboleth ' from

[1] *The Idea of a Christian Society* (London, 1939), IV.

the famous Old Testament story[2] became a term indicating narrow-mindedness. The Old Testament narrator did not understand it in this way. He knew that a society has a right to safeguard itself by standards, and a church by dogmas. The Bible is set down in the midst of the Church as the Church's ' shibboleth '. Here is to be found what is essential in her character. In a sense then the Church, in the person of her individual members and clergy, may be very imperfect and yet still be true to her essential character and function.

Nevertheless everyone is conscious of the tension between the Church's profession—even her dogmas—and the practice of her individual members; and most of all the minister, whose calling is to speak of truth and conduct, must frequently be troubled by the thought of inconsistency.

Luther was acutely aware of the problem involved in this duality. He is gloriously certain of the absolute authority of the Church's proclamation, making the point that when the Church prays 'forgive us our trespasses' it is not its proclamation for which it asks forgiveness; 'for doctrine is not our doing but God's own Word which can neither sin nor do wrong. For a preacher must not say the Lord's Prayer, nor ask forgiveness of sins, when he has preached (if he is a true preacher), but must confess and exult with Jeremiah: Lord, Thou knowest that what has gone forth from my mouth is right and pleasing to Thee . . . For it is not my word but God's . . .'

Luther acknowledges that the preacher may well feel timidity. 'Such timidity arises from the fact that we earnestly believe that God's Word is such a splendid, majestic thing, that we know ourselves all too unworthy that such a great thing should be spoken and done through us, who still live in flesh and blood. But our adversaries, the devils, hordes of papists and all the world, are joyful and undaunted; in their great holiness they presume impudently to say: Here is

[1] Judges xii.

God; we are the ministers, prophets and apostles of God's
Church, just as all false prophets have always done . . . But
humility and fear in God's Word has at all times been the
true mark of the true Church, boldness and audacity in
human arrogance has been the true mark of devils, as indeed
cannot but be noticed manifestly even in the Pope's
" decretals " . . .'[1]

It is clear from all this that there are elements of moral
tension inherent in any conception of the Church and of the
preacher's office that is realistic, just as there are elements
of tension in every situation in life that is real and not merely
theoretical or romantically conceived. The human plight
which required an Incarnation in the reign of Caesar Augus-
tus required also, in this present age between advent and
advent, a Church (which is another kind of Incarnation), and
in that Church ministers of the Word in sermon and sacraments. Such ministers are certainly not mechanical mouth-
pieces like the loud-speaker of a gramophone, safeguarded
from error or futility by *ex opere operato* insurance. They
are certainly men exercising human judgement and before
God taking responsibility for it.

This responsibility is lifted on to a very high level in the
Reformed Churches, where the minister's duty to *preach* is
enjoined much more categorically than in other communions,
and the very freedom he enjoys to arrange the order of
service in his parish church lays him wide open, if he be
careless or ill-advised, to every possibility of spiritual and
pastoral error.

The mouth-piece then may utter the message. After ordin-
ation the minister is indeed in ' holy orders '; as Forsyth said,
he is ' a sacramental person '. The mouth-piece may also so
blur or otherwise qualify the message that the Word of God
be made ' of none effect '. He cannot escape from the chal-

[1] From *Wider Hans Worst*, 1541, quoted by Karl Barth, *Church
Dogmatics* (Edinburgh, 1956), Vol. i, ch. IV, pp. 747 ff.

lenge of this duality. This is why there is no room for pride in the ministry, nor for lack of humour which is a sense of proportion, nor for the closed mind. As Daniel Jenkins puts it, we are 'the Master's apprentices'.

How far does the fact that the Word is humanly shaped and presented ('we have this treasure in earthen vessels'[1]) limit God? Or how far does God over-rule the limitations of human experience, skill, devotion, and good sense, so that the eternal Word may survive the human utterance? This question is the burden that lies upon the heart of the minister.

The burden is part of our appointed discipline. So long as we are aware of it, we shall never take this ministry lightly and cease to apply ourselves to those other disciplines which are essential to ministry in any age and never more so than now, the disciplines of study, devotion, preaching, and pastoral techniques. Of Bengel, the commentator, it was said that he went to his desk as to an altar, and so, if preaching is to be sacramental, must we. Of Hubert Kelly, founder of the Anglican community at Kelham, it is recorded that when a Japanese was asked the secret of Kelly's extraordinary influence in Japan, he replied that it was because he was 'a holy man'. Not first a scholar or administrator, but a 'holy man'.

What was implied by the term 'holy' (like 'sanctity' it has lost its proper connotation in the West) was that element of spiritual authority which a prophet was felt to possess when he said: 'Thus saith the Lord.'[2] He was a man who knew what God thought. For, once more, a preacher's effectiveness does not depend primarily upon his personal virtues; if it did, who would dare open his mouth? The

[1] 2 Cor. iv. 7.
[2] Cf. what was said of seventeenth-century Alexander Henderson by a brother minister: 'I love you, sir, because I think you are a man in whom I see much of the image of Christ, and who fears God'. *Vide* Sheriff Orr's *Alexander Henderson* (London, 1919), p. 379.

preacher can only confess as Luther confessed when, during a plague, they asked him: 'Are you not afraid?' and he replied: 'I am not St. Paul, I am only lecturing on him!' Many a preacher, like Luther, has been a quite imperfect man yet a mighty force for good because, in spite of obvious imperfections of temperament or character, people knew he was fundamentally right in heart towards God and dedicated.

It is also true, fortunately for the Church's witness, that the sacramental efficacy of preaching does not depend most on intellectual capacity or scholarship. No doubt many a saving sermon has been preached without them. Formal truth in the mouth of a good man will stand a good deal of hauling about and even a good deal of mauling. On the other hand, which of us has never heard a truth, stated with formal accuracy, turned into something like a ghastly lie in the moment of utterance simply by a tone of voice? Nevertheless we are not taught in our theological colleges to despise learning. The acquisition of scholarship is not a luxury the busy minister can afford himself only after everything else is done. It is a duty such that, if he fails in it, his other duties will be to some extent unskilfully done, however much they may be popularly applauded by those who do not know what is required. Scholarship is an apparatus for bringing out the truth of Scripture and thus safeguarding the Church against all that is not of Christ. It is one of the means of conditioning the mouth-piece to speak the Word of the eternal God.

Nevertheless neither scholarship nor personal merits count for much in the end unless learning is an instrument in the hands of a man who has the stamp of 'holiness' or 'set-apartness' that the Church's orders confer, and unless the personal 'merits' be the fruits of this 'holiness'—of Christ's doing alone.

Stemming from this consideration of first principles, let us select some of the essential marks of Christian preaching, not by way of completing the subject as if it were intended to be a treatise on homiletic techniques, but by way of developing something of the particular burden and recall of these chapters. Two of the marks, which the pulpit requires to recover or to develop today, are Biblical concreteness or realism in thought and talk, and a certain note of austerity or Christian challenge.

### III. BIBLICAL CONCRETENESS

The preacher requires always to steer between the Scylla of scholasticism and the Charybdis of illuminism. Scholasticism has been defined as ' the letter without the Spirit ' and illuminism as ' the Spirit without the letter '. Clearly both are wrong. The one is as liable to be bloodless as the other is to be undisciplined or idiosyncratic.

For a time in recent theological history it appeared as if there might be a danger of a return to something like scholasticism through the revival of the Reformed theology. Some of those who faithfully submitted themselves to the disciplines of the new Biblical studies were in danger of evading the difficult task of presentation. They were content to work out, according to sound exegetical rules, what a Scripture text actually said, thereafter what the inspired writer understood it to mean in his day (this necessarily involving study of the corresponding Old Testament thought-forms), and finally seeking to discover what God was saying through this Scripture to modern men and women. All this however, without painfully seeking to commend the doctrine, an office which was supposed to be that of the Holy Spirit in his inner witness as the Word was preached.

It is possible, however, for one preacher to throw down before a congregation the doctrine of justification by faith in a series of unpalatable propositions using a vocabulary which gives new and highly technical meaning to such words as 'occurrence', 'event', and 'possibility', and for Jesus to seem very far away; while another preacher with a quarter the resources but twice the understanding of God's gracious ways with men—his strange and beautiful *oikonomia* or domestic management of them—may, without ever uttering the term 'justification', so preach that the hearer is led into the Presence of the Most High and knows himself to be (though he may not use the word) 'justified', given standing with God in time and eternity. One preacher thinks of 'justification' as a *doctrine*. Another knows it to be the gracious act of God.

When Sir William Petty sent Pepys a proposed publication of his studies, statistical and economic, his covering note contained the sentences:

The matters pretend good to all the King's subjects and the means propounded are of an high extraordinary nature, and therefore should be exposed to public view. . . . If you cannot understand them alone, they are not fit for the public and must be made plainer.[1]

Every word of this is applicable to preaching. In the present condition of general theological innocence it is the solidly concrete language of the Bible that constitutes the preacher's lively ally rather than the abstract conceptions of the study. The psalms do not smell of the lamp (excepting perhaps the acrostics); they are the prayers of ordinary folk in every kind of emergency or happy fulfilment, of the sick, the imprisoned, those in peril of the ocean, soldiers, exiles, men and women asking questions about God, facing death or temptation, or confessing sin.[2]

It is important to note that the distinction is not between two kinds of language but between two kinds of thinking.

[1] 8 Sept., 1687; quoted by Arthur Bryant, *Pepys: The Saviour of the Navy* (London and Glasgow, 1949), p. 205.

[2] *Vide* George Gunn, *God in the Psalms* (Edinburgh, 1956), ch. 1 ff.

The average reader today and sometimes even the preacher himself misses the force of the Bible's universal concreteness because he himself reads into its text those abstract conceptions which are characteristic of modern thought-modes; such modes are not to be discovered in the Bible but can only be *imported* into its interpretation.

Modern studies have served to reveal even more fully than before how thoroughgoing is this Biblical concreteness. Just as in the Old Testament to speak of a man 'knowing' a woman implies an actual physical relationship, so when Simon Peter denies Jesus, saying 'I know not the man', it is fully understood by those to whom he speaks what he is saying; he is not saying that he has never heard of Jesus but that he is not on any kind of personal terms with him at all.[1] In quite the same way, in the Bible the 'knowledge of God' does not signify belief in the form of accepting propositions or making a catalogue of the divine attributes; it implies some kind of personal relationship such as is implied in Bultmann's saying that 'to believe means not to have apprehended but to have been apprehended'.[2] In logical converse to this, within the covers of the Bible a man's doubts do not mean that he questions God's existence but that he is not sure whether God is going to be good and gracious to him. They are, so to speak, believer's doubts.

This distinction still exists. Modern abstract doubt (no longer a European or American phenomenon) is illustrated in the experience of Mildred Cable and Francesca and Evangeline French, held up at a frontier post in Central Asia, and camping in the darkness, to whom through the blackness of the night came the voice of the sentry: 'Tell me, you holy women, is there a God? If so, he must be senseless and cruel to permit such things as we have seen.' How different the

[1] *Vide* Th. C. Vriezen, *An Outline of Old Testament Theology* (Oxford, 1958).
[2] *Kerugma and Myth* (ed. H. W. Bartsch, London, 1953), ch. II, p. 21.

confession of Ludwig Steil, the German pastor writing in his diary in a Nazi prison camp on 11 November, 1944:

Last night I lay awake for an hour and had many questions to put to God. They were posed not in a spirit of challenge, but only out of longing for an answer. And suddenly the verses of a long-forgotten hymn sung in East Berlin rang in my ears and silenced me: 'Oh, that thou couldst believe, then wouldst thou wonders see, for by thy side for evermore, thy Saviour then would be.'[1]

The difference is between the doubt that asks questions about God and that (and it is the Biblical way) which asks questions of God.

Illustrations of this Biblical concrete way of thinking abound even though, because of the difficulty of language as well as of modern habits of thought, they are readily missed in reading the Bible. In the Old Testament 'to hear the Word of God' (*shama*) implies not only hearing with the ear but something more like 'attending' and 'understanding': if a man can be said to have 'heard the Word of God' the implication is that he has agreed to obey.[2] In some tribal languages which have remained uninfluenced by the abstractions of Western culture, there is no means of making a verbal distinction between the idea of believing and that of obeying. The one word carries the double sense, and corresponds to the Biblical way of thinking, which finds faithful expression in Kierkegaard's: 'It is so difficult to believe because it is so difficult to obey.' The Bible accepts the fact that belief and obedience are two things which God has joined together and man cannot separate.

It is not at all surprising, in view of all this, that the all-pervasive term 'the Word' (O.T. *dabar*, N.T. *logos*) carries

[1] L. Steil, in *Dying we Live*, ed. Käthe Kuhn (Harvill, 1956), p. 87.
[2] *Vide* Alan Richardson, *Introduction to the Theology of the New Testament* (London, 1958), p. 30.

the sense also of something being *done:* 'He sent His Word and healed them' (Ps. cvii. 20). 'The Word became flesh' (John i. 14).

Translation sometimes masks this concrete way of thinking. In Exod. ix. 27, Pharaoh's speech: 'The Lord is righteous, and I and my people are wicked', suggests to the average reader that Pharaoh is pondering the attributes of Israel's God. What he is actually saying is something like: 'God has delivered judgement (vindicated Israel); we therefore (the Egyptians) are in the wrong.'

Joubert (Matthew Arnold's 'a French Coleridge') well understood this quality of concreteness in the preacher's thought and utterance: 'In things that are visible and palpable, never prove what is believed already; in things that are certain and mysterious—mysterious by their greatness and by their nature—make people believe them, and do not prove them; in things that are matters of practice and duty, command, and do not explain.'[1] On the preacher's side the difference is between reading a lecture and being the mouth-piece of the Word of God.

On the hearer's side the difference is between hearing a sermon and hearing the Word of God: between seeing forked lightning on a film, and being exposed to the whip and terror of the thing itself: between reading an article about life in the army and being handed your call-up papers: between discussing a dogma and meeting the living God.

All living and tested experience protests that this is the preacher's business and this the manner of doing it. Had entrance into the Church's ministry required and implied nothing more, and nothing less, than intellectual certitude in the form of abstract propositions, it is quite certain that the present volume would never have been written. For if this (as St. Paul also saw as applying to the keeping of the Law) were the grounds of acceptance by God and of a man's own

[1] Matthew Arnold, *Critical Essays*, loc. cit.

acceptance of the ministry, who should be called at all? Doubt as to one iota in the form and language of the Creed would mean doubt as to the whole system of belief—' unfaith in aught is want of faith in all '. And in such a mood of uncertainty many of us who are now in the middle years of ministry once stood at the threshold of life, perplexed about belief and still more perplexed about ministry.

And yet—we are here, in orders. Looking back we can see now more clearly than we could at the time the truth of Dr. John Baillie's saying about people who believe in the bottom of their hearts what they deny with the top of their minds; and looking back we can see more clearly now than we could then, that at a profounder level than that of formal perplexities as to matters of faith was an inescapable impression of being claimed by one whom we could either obey or disobey. 'God led me ', said Luther, 'like an old blind horse.' Later, some of us came to understand other things, and this among them, that the faculty of reason which we had so greatly prized and so inadequately learned to employ, was not an immediate instrument for the apprehension of ultimate truths (valuable as it is and active as it ought to be even in worship) but was an instrument for the verification of insights otherwise given and certified. For there is a sense in which God is not to be known in his ultimate and unthinkable majesty, the important thing being that one should acknowledge the experience of being known by God. St. Paul is content so to state it: 'Then shall I know even as also I am known ' (1 Cor. xiii. 12). This does not dispense with the necessity of mental fight; it implies it, but certainly assumes that the mental fight takes place within the experience of encounter.

This is the concreteness of the Bible's thought, attitude, and language. It is an essential characteristic of preaching. Preaching is the Word in action and the preacher is the mouth-piece. Here, where the Word is spoken, God meets with man, and there is a clash or a marriage of wills. It is as concrete as that.

## IV. SACRAMENTS ALSO ARE AN ACTION—OF GOD

The sacraments also, if they are not to degenerate—it is the peril inherent in them—into superstitions, require to be understood as God's *action* towards his Church. 'The essence of all religion', wrote Troeltsch, 'is not the dogma or idea, but the cultus and communion.' Clearly it is more, but it is also this; and this cultus is, *essentially*, not an unalterable sequence of verbal forms but an action. The word spoken, if it be the vehicle of the eternal Word, is itself an action. Something is said and ritually done and in the doing of it something happens which could not happen except through the action of Christ in the Church through the sacraments of his own appointing. If we do not believe this, we do not believe in sacraments.

It is at this point that the sectaries have appeared to part from the Church as reformed, which adhered to that primitive catholicity which was still basically Scriptural and uncorrupted. It will not be gainsaid that Puritanism in the process of decline proceeded from over-valuing the emotional by-product of prayer to seek that by-product as an end in itself. Certainly it under-valued any process of worship from which this element was conspicuously missing, tending to assume the emotion to be a reliable warranty of Christ's presence.

This emphasis is still reflected in the type of prayer which begins: 'Lord help us to feel Thy Presence . . .'—a species of formulation not altogether desirable even for private devotion, reflecting as it does the troubled mind of our age, and certainly utterly unfitted for the corporate prayer of the believing Church. In the classical liturgies as in the best liturgies of the reformed branches of the Church, it is not man's feeling that matters but God's attitude to us. Reverse this order and the error becomes a dangerous one. When the means of worship are used as a means of inducing emotion, the uninstructed will do exactly what they are thereby taught to do, regard emotion as the end of worship and stop short of the Divine Will. The Holy Communion is not an expression of the Church's devout hope that something good may happen. It is Christ's operative action in which something of eternal significance does actually happen.[1]

As to what that something is—whose mouth-piece the celebrant is, Christ's or the people's or both—remains the question in the high debate which unhappily continues between the Roman Church and the Church as reformed.

Both hold an operative view of the Sacrament, the Roman Church even to the point of a ritual (yet literal) slaying. A Lenten sermon of 1884, almost shocking in carrying the sacrificial theory of the Blessed Sacrament to its logical conclusion, bids the people picture the priest at the altar giving life to the elements in the act of consecration and at the same moment by the ritual word slaying the eternal Victim, thus:

The Son of God is there, and he dies a mystical death. What power, my God, Thou hast given to thy priests. . . . Their word has become an instrument more pointed and trenchant than the knife which slaughtered the victims of the ancient law. . . . Christ continues to live beneath the mortal blow, and yet he gives expression, so far as in him lies, to the state of death and destruction proper to sacrifice. He gives expression to this by the total eclipse of his glory, by the captivity of his sacred members and of his movements *under the eucharistic species*, by the cessation of natural functions which are proper to his senses: obscurity, immobility, silence, annihilation, which

---

[1] According to Reformed standards, the sacraments are *acts of God* which are at once declaratory of the Gospel and instrumental in its application. The high sacramental doctrine of the Church as reformed is indicated by the basilican posture of the minister in celebrating.

place him at our disposition to such an extent that we can treat him as inert matter, a mysterious state which he has only assumed that he might become our nourishment, and results, therefore, in the destruction of his sacramental being, which is the consummation of the sacrifice.[1]

From this error have stemmed many others, including the use of monstrance and all the furniture of reservation (so far as it is employed not for later communication but for devotional purposes as the object of adoration). The brood of errors is conditioned, if not generated, by the emphasis upon the substance of bread and wine to the virtual exclusion of an essential emphasis upon the action in the Blessed Sacrament, the offering (of God's gifts—'these thine own gifts of bread and wine'), fraction, consecration, distribution, and reception. In the nature of the case, the greater the stress upon substance viewed as the materials of sacrifice susceptible of metaphysical change, the less the stress upon Christ's living action within the Church and the greater the stress upon the intermediary, the officiating priest.[2]

The difference is radical between a supposedly sacrificial Eucharist or Holy Communion and that in which Christ's minister stands behind the Holy Table (the primitive

[1] Quoted from P. Monsabre by E. B. Koenker, *The Liturgical Renaissance in the Roman Catholic Church* (U.S.A., 1954), ch. VII.

[2] Hooker had no special objection to the use of the word *priest*, for the not very strong reason (though it was a very practical one) that now the idea of sacrifice in the Sacrament was no longer held and the once suggestive title of priest no longer conveyed the idea that the Eucharist was to be understood as a sacrifice. Like Calvin (who however read a solid sense of *episkopos* into the term[(a)]) Hooker thought other terms than priest, such as ' presbyter ', preferable— ' more fit, and in propriety of speech more agreeable than priest with the drift of the whole Gospel of Jesus Christ '. *Ecclesiastical Polity*, v. lxxviii, 2, 3. On this *vide* James Moffatt, *The Presbyterian Churches* (London, 1928), ch. VIII.

[(a)] Institutes, Bk. IV, ch. III, 8.

'basilican posture') 'in Christ's stead'. This emphasis was stated in its radical form by Forsyth, who contended that the symbolism of the Holy Communion '*did not lie in the elements but in the action,* the entire action—word and deed. It lay in action first on Christ's part, then on the part of the Church'. 'It was the *action* that was symbolical, the breaking rather than the bread, the outpouring rather than the wine. "This" is not this object but this act. Remove the comma after "body". "This is my body broken" . . . So with the cup . . . "This is my blood shed".'[1] Because it is not primarily the elements but the action that is significant, Christ therefore is not 'inert matter at our disposal'. He is the Real Presence, the Invisible Host, taking action by breaking bread and pouring the cup in the midst of the Church in the sacrament of the New Covenant. The minister is the hand of Christ in that breaking. He is the mouth-piece when he speaks the word: 'This do in remembrance of Me', as truly as when he says: 'Hear the Word of God.' Nowhere in liturgical or theological history is it possible to find a 'higher' doctrine of Church and of sacraments than this which is the characteristic feature of the Church as reformed.

The concreteness of the Word in sermon and sacraments is necessary if a second essential characteristic of Christian preaching is to be effectual—that is, the note of Christian challenge.

V. THE NOTE OF CHRISTIAN CHALLENGE

A preaching or a service of worship which lacks the quality

[1] P. T. Forsyth, *The Church and the Sacraments* (2nd ed. London, 1947), ch. XII. Forsyth held a too exclusive stress upon the substance to be the 'lame foot of Anglicanism' as it had been 'the defect of the Chalcedonian mind'. But he thought that what was necessary was not the discarding but the moralizing of Chalcedonism, 'the conversion of its metaphysic (i.e. its mental habit) from thinking of underlying substance to think of energy and ethic'.

of challenge—which does not include the severity and the love of God—is false to the Gospel and, since such misrepresentations always occur together, it is false to life. Therefore it has nothing to offer people.

Here as in everything else we must stand on the edge of the crowd in Galilee and learn before we can properly preach. In the Gospel picture our Lord who was 'full homely to us' offered a rich sympathy, but it was a sympathy that never softened because it never evaded; it was a sympathy that fortified people. It is told of a girl who returned from a consultation with her doctor that, having learned that she would suffer permanently from a disability which, it seemed, would be seriously crippling to the Christian work on which she had set her heart, she was near to breaking point. Telling her spiritual adviser, a wise and experienced woman, of this, and no doubt expecting sympathy, she was astonished to receive the reply, 'Very well then, we shall make it an offering and not an execution.' At that unexpected, spiritually sound, and tonic response, she was instantly braced and thereafter faced the challenge of difficulty with a steady heart.

A minister, discovering very quickly how many people in his congregation and parish require to learn to make friends with difficult duty, discovers also that sentimentality can never take the place of truth. Embedded in the larger story of Palm Sunday is a subsidiary story of an unknown disciple in an unnamed village who had a colt which Jesus needed and who gave it willingly. It was to be found, the disciples were told, in 'the village over against you', where people do not expect to find romance. Courage is required to live greatly in 'the village over against you'. That is where significant issues are being fought; and it is to people whose lot is cast in very ordinary settings as a rule, but whose lives are important to themselves and to God, that we have to preach. They also have to learn, as we who preach have to learn, that duty done reluctantly remains a burden, while duty done as a service to Christ and his Kingdom becomes a kind of sacrament.

This, preaching with the note of high challenge, is what people are waiting for, though they may not know they have been waiting for it until they hear it. When they do, they have the feeling of coming home, of entering into the world of reality after trying to make a home for themselves in the world of illusion.[1] André Maurois was profoundly right in saying: 'To cater to the public is to disappoint it.' This is true also of preaching; to offer people what they want, or what they think they want, is to disappoint them. It is even possible for people to flatter a preacher for a popular utterance and, on reflection, to feel vaguely cheated.

There is a magnificent Old Testament story (1 Kings xi) which describes how Hadad, an exile from his native Judah, finds shelter with royal Pharaoh in Egypt, and is loaded with all the things people spend so much of their life seeking; he is given a roof over his head, victuals, land, and presumably a suitably royal pension. For a time he believes in his own happiness, imagining he has settled for good. But one day there blows into his comfortable palace on a stray wind the merest breath of a rumour to the effect that David his enemy, the occasion of his exile, is dead; and in a trice every fibre of Hadad's mind is quivering as he thinks of his lost throne. Nothing will serve but he must go out into the unknown, precarious future. Pharaoh is at a loss: 'What hast thou lacked with me that thou seekest to go to thine own country?' He had a house, hadn't he?—and a competence and much else besides. But he lacked the spice of danger. He lacked the ineradicable joy of pitting all that was finest in him against the odds which are always present in any life that is real, as contrasted with the life that the triflers, the charlatans, and the timid dream about. He lacked that particular species of happiness that Napoleon described as 'the

[1] As to this point, *vide* earlier chapters also.

fullest employment of my talents'. He yearned for the sight of his own bare hills and the Spartan economy of a small people living always on the edge of the whirlwind. He lacked nothing at all—nothing—except those few essential things that make life real life and redeem it from being a mere continuity of days. The preacher who wants 'preaching points' would say that at least three suggest themselves from the story: that over against the natural human desire for security, there needs to be allowed room in every life for chivalrous adventure, and Christ offers it; that over against the natural human desire for an easy goal, the need is for a new, usually difficult, but better start, and, in his own rich way, Christ offers it; and that over against the natural desire for freedom, the need is for one to whom to account, and Christ offers it in his own Person. Even Hadad needed a Master, and for him God was in Jerusalem, not Egypt.

Christ deals with people in *his* own way, not theirs. It is relatively easy to preach from the words in our Lord's description of the Good Shepherd and the sheep. 'They shall be saved, and shall go in and out, and find pasture' under the heads of 'security, liberty, and sufficiency', suggesting, in the familiar pattern of 'popular' Christianity, that in Christ the world would find all these, its passionate ideals and desires, fulfilled. But is it true? Can an interpretation of such a passage be in fact the Gospel if it bear no 'print of the nails'?

The commentary, not on the passage quoted, but on the usual kind of exposition of it, is to be found in the story of our Lord's 'temptation', or testing in the Wilderness, where the Adversary's proposals (the Old Testament references had Messianic significance for our Lord's people) were for bread, security, and glory of a certain sort. What was missing? There was no mention of judgement, of sin, of forgiveness, of love, of neighbour, no challenge of great things and to great things.

'Mankind', says Reinhold Niebuhr, 'is led by hunger

and by dreams.' It is true. The planners of welfare states know, and are right in knowing, one half of that truth. Perhaps it is not their business to remember about the dreams. But it is the preacher's business, lest God 'give men their desire and send leanness into their souls'. For the hunger and the dreams both require to be defined. Mankind in the ordinary cannot define his own hungers; the preacher has to do it for him. Christ does not, as even preachers have too frequently asserted, meet man's needs. He alters them. After a man has met Christ, he finds his needs have changed. He needs forgiveness; he needs a task; he needs someone to love in Christ's Name; he needs to be made at home in the Unseen. By his coming Christ meets the needs that this same coming provokes. After this, 'all these other things', the gracious gifts of God in the natural world, 'shall be added unto you' in God's way and time and measure. This is the austerity and the love of God, and all else in preaching and in common prayer is sentimentality and betrayal.

## VI. 'MULTITUDES IN THE VALLEY OF DECISION'

In a volume of memoirs John G. Winant,[1] who was the United States ambassador to the Court of St. James's at the time of the Battle of Britain, drew a dramatic picture of the scene in the operations room at Uxbridge when Winston Churchill was there during the closing phase of that epoch-shaping air duel. The Prime Minister sat with Air Vice-Marshal Park during what, looking back, we now know to have been moments of destiny. The endless waves of German bombers came over and in reply Park put in more and more fighter squadrons.

At length Churchill asked: 'How many more have you got?' and the Air Vice-Marshal replied: 'I am putting in my last.'

[1] *Letter from Grosvenor Square* (London, 1947), ch. IV, p. 29.

'They waited', wrote Winant, 'for the next German wave. It never came. The Germans too had put in *their* last.'

Our study in these chapters has come full circle. How far is this present age, in the second half of the twentieth century, a moment of destiny for the Christian future? We are not able to tell. We know only that the story we have just quoted is not an unworthy, or unfair, analogy of the situation in which the word of preaching and the words of common prayer and praise are uttered. There are souls in conflict and there is conflict in souls. Simon Peter, Judas, Pilate, Herod, Saul on the Damascus Road, in fact all who parade themselves before our eyes as the Bible is opened, read, and preached, these are with superficial differences figures of today. To such we preach, believing that, in preaching, Christ is engaged in his conflict—his *agonia*.[1]

Some, as in the Bible, are facing moral issues, ill-equipped for that struggle, not because they have not been 'decently brought up' (the moral wreckage of today is the same in every class of society), but because they are utterly without ultimate discernment.

It is this theological discernment which lies at the heart of any proclamation that is going to have anything vital to say to the condition of society at this moment in the long story of man. Moral exhortation is always the weakest form of preaching, just as the announcement of objective facts is always the strongest. It is a gospel we preach, and that, by very definition, is 'news'—it is 'news of reality.'

News of reality? Charles Morgan, quoting and discussing a phrase of Sir Maurice Bowra, says that 'art is never a medicine to heal an age. It is "news of reality" expressed in symbols, joys, incantations, enchantments, and the age that

---

[1] 'Think with thyself that the devil was as busy as thou wast, when thou wast preaching.'—Thomas Boston, op. cit., p. 87.

cannot read it fails to synthesise its disparate experiences and is " lost in the crowd ".[1]

If this can be said even of art, that, within its own restricted and mitigated understanding of its function, it is ' news of reality ', how much more can it be said of this dramatic story of God's dealings with men from the symbol of primal creation in the Book of Genesis to the clear-sounding eschatological hope in the New Testament, that it is ' news of reality ' expressed in symbols, joys, enchantments, and above all (for this is the nature of the Christian revelation) in the ' mighty acts ' of God in his dealings with men; and without the understanding of life that this story offers, men can make nothing of their ' disparate experiences ', and must be ' lost in the crowd '.

Yet even to say this does not express the sovereign and essential distinction which marks Christian preaching and common prayer from everything else which attempts to offer a explanation of this mysterious life of ours; and that sovereign distinction is this, that in song, liturgy, and preaching, what the Church experiences is not ' news of reality ' or, more explicitly, news of God himself: it is actual encounter.

[1] Essay on ' The heritage of symbolism ' in *Reflections in a Mirror* (London, 1944).

# APPENDIX

## AN ORDER OF PUBLIC WORSHIP

Conformable with the primitive eucharistic pattern and with
the worship of the Church as reformed, enriched as to detail.
The people's part is indicated by *italics*.

### I. 'LET US WORSHIP GOD'

Corresponding to
*the liturgy of the
catechumens,*
otherwise called
*the liturgy of the
Word.*

*Hymn* (God in creation etc., or for morning, or for
    recollection, or an 'office hymn')
Call to prayer (the people standing)
Prayers of humble approach,
        of confession of sin: general (particular)
    LORD HAVE MERCY UPON US
  ℞ *Christ have mercy upon us*
    *Lord have mercy upon us.*
Absolution (a Scriptural declaration of forgiveness)
Prayer for help and/or *a hymn* (e.g. of the Holy
    Spirit)

### II. 'HEAR THE WORD OF GOD'

Old Testament
Epistle
*Gradual psalm*, sung (or spoken responsively)
Gospel
*The Apostles' Creed* (or later, following the Sermon)
Prayers: for illumination and for the Church and/or
    *hymn* or anthem (for illumination or on the theme
    of lections and sermon)
' IN THE NAME OF THE FATHER ' etc.
The Sermon
Ascription of glory

### III. 'LIFT UP YOUR HEARTS'

LIFT UP YOUR HEARTS

Corresponding to
*the liturgy of the
faithful,*
otherwise called
*the liturgy of the
Upper Room.*

℞ *We lift them up unto the Lord*

LET US GIVE THANKS UNTO OUR LORD GOD

℞ *It is meet and right so to do.*

Thanksgiving, adoration, and 'remembrance' of
Christ (in forms of prayer and/or such songs of the
Church as *Te Deum, Sanctus, Benedictus* or a
*hymn* of adoration)

Prayers of intercession: *Lord's Prayer*

The Offerings

Dedication of the offerings and of ourselves, with
remembrance of the communion of saints.

GLORY BE TO THE FATHER

℞ *And to the Son, and to the Holy Ghost* etc. . . .

*Hymn* (of praise or for close of worship)

The Benediction

# INDEX

*Printed in Great Britain by*
*Northumberland Press Limited*
*Gateshead on Tyne*

# DATE DUE

| | | | |
|---|---|---|---|
| | | | |
| | | | |
| | | | |
| | | | |
| | | | |
| | | | |
| | | | |
| | | | |
| | | | |
| | | | |
| | | | |
| | | | |
| | | | |
| | | | |
| | | | |
| | | | |
| | | | |
| | | | |
| GAYLORD | | | PRINTED IN U.S.A. |